emily
A CHILD IN HEAVEN

overcoming the loss

of a stillborn child

emily
A CHILD IN HEAVEN

Deborah Lycett

Authentic
LIFESTYLE

First published 2004 by Authentic Lifestyle, an imprint of
Authentic Media, 9 Holdom Avenue, Bletchley, Milton Keynes,
MK1 1QR and
P.O. Box 1047, Waynesboro, GA 30830-2047, USA.

British Library Cataloguing in Publication Data
A catalogue record for this book is available from the British
Library

1-86024-443-2

Cover design by David Lund
Print Management by Adare Carwin
Printed and Bound in Denmark by Nørhaven Paperback

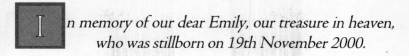

*I*n memory of our dear Emily, our treasure in heaven, who was stillborn on 19th November 2000.

'Do not store up for yourselves treasures on earth, where moth and rust destroy,
and where thieves break in and steal. But store up for yourselves treasures in heaven,
where moth and rust do not destroy, and where thieves do not break in and steal.
For where your treasure is, there your heart will be also.'
Matthew 6:19–21

'There is a time for everything, and a season for every activity under heaven:
a time to be born and a time to die . . .
a time to weep and a time to laugh, a time to mourn and a time to dance . . . .
He has made everything beautiful in its time. He has also set eternity in the hearts of men . . . ' *Ecclesiastes 3:1,2,4,11*

For Abigail, when you ask and Izzy, when you need to know.

ACKNOWLEDGEMENTS

With thanks to my husband, Tim, for all his patience and encouragement and to my mother, Elizabeth Gray, who has been a sympathetic ear and loving counsel. Not forgetting my dad, Norman, whose support and comments helped greatly. Thank you to Margaret for your help and for being such a good friend. Thank you to Malcolm, Sheila, Liz, Zoë, Peter, Louise, David and all those at Authentic Media who have worked so hard to make the publication of this book possible. Most of all, thank you to God, who has been my strength and my inspiration. This is for his glory. I pray that all who read it will be touched by the immense love he has for them.

CONTENTS

PROLOGUE

❦

I was a successful person. Someone who had dreams and ambitions that always seemed to work out. My friends would look at me and think, 'She's got it made. Always had everything she's ever wanted, always succeeded at whatever she put her hand to. Such an easy life.'

I was bright, always did well at school. A 'C' grade was a failure to me and a 'B' meant I wasn't very good at something. I was only ever satisfied with 'A's. I got a first class honours degree at university and two weeks after that walked into a happy marriage, secure home and a graduate position was waiting for me on my return from honeymoon.

My first child came easily two years later and my life changed somewhat as I was thrown into the responsibility of parenthood. Then two and a half years after that, my 'perfect' world was shattered . . .

1

THAT JUST WOULDN'T HAPPEN TO ME, NOT ME

❧

I felt uneasy. I wasn't sure if Emily was moving. In fact over the last few days movements seemed to have lessened. Perhaps it was just that Braxton Hicks contractions had taken their place; these tightenings of my tummy had now become quite strong. After all, movements do change towards the end of pregnancy, don't they?

'So maybe, just maybe, Emily will be early.' I do so hate the wait at the end of a pregnancy; each hour from your due date seems like a hundred years. Abigail had been five days late. That was two and a half years ago now; my patience had expired and just as I resigned myself to the fact that she would never come, the contractions began. I had been ready well in advance and had been doing jigsaw puzzles to pass the time. Now it was Emily's turn. I was all ready; everything was done and I had an urge to keep washing the kitchen floor even though there were still two weeks to go.

'She could come this weekend,' I thought, 'I'm ready for her now.'

We had named her Emily, meaning 'eager', after we saw how active she was, bouncing around during her

twenty week scan. Her middle name was Ruth, after the
Ruth in the Bible who was a faithful friend to Naomi.
Emily, we hoped, would be a faithful friend to Abigail.
When we were pondering on her name, Tim sealed the
decision by putting on the song 'Emily' by All About Eve
and we played it to Fred and Margaret one Friday
evening – we had met Fred and Margaret at church some
five years ago now and we had become firm friends.

Fred is French, stocky and balding. He is a cartoonist
and he and my husband Tim share the same sense of
humour and receding hairline. Margaret teaches
English to foreign students and is also fluent in French.
We have often heard them switch into French conversation and if Tim and I didn't know them so well, we
might feel offended. Margaret and I share a passion for
soppy videos and sweets. We often plan an evening that
begins with making a sugary snack. Toffee crispy cakes
are a favourite; we melt the bright green, blue and
orange marshmallows in a saucepan and watch the
colours swirl into brown sticky 'goo'. Then we settle
down to enjoy munching our way through a film, while
we send the men out. You would never guess from
these treats that I am a dietitian, or that Margaret and I
are slim. Well, I am usually slim; now my oval face had
filled out to a fat round and my distended stomach
meant I could no longer see my feet, let alone touch my
toes. Margaret was filling out, too: she was now six
months pregnant.

We usually spent Friday nights together. Since we had
moved to the other side of town a year ago we decided to
schedule in our meeting as we could no longer talk to
each other over the back garden fence.

Today was Friday and I had had one of those days
when life seems perfect and everything is wonderful. I

had this feeling of complete euphoria. I had spent a relaxing morning at an indoor soft play area with Abigail. I sat and read a little, while Abigail slid time and time again down an enormous blue slide, and was buried underneath a mass of soft foam balls.

In the evening Fred and Margaret came over. We were in our living room, all four of us squashed on to our three-seater sofa, although Tim and Fred were more balanced on the arms while we two pregnant women sank into the comfort of the cushions. We were watching *Friends* on the TV, but my mind was wandering. I felt a little odd and said to Margaret, 'I think I'm having contractions, but it might just be Emily moving. Look, feel there, what do you think?'

Margaret put her hand on the top of my tummy and shrugged; she wasn't sure either. As time progressed I felt more and more concerned. That night, I slept badly, anxiously trying to feel Emily move; again all I felt were mild contractions. I nearly woke Tim to tell him 'I think we might have our baby this weekend,' but I decided to wait and see. I woke in the night, Abigail needed her potty; as I got back into bed, I felt cold. I lay huddled, shivering under the duvet, trying to get warm.

'That's strange,' I thought, 'I'm always so hot.' And then I fell asleep. The next morning I said to Tim, 'Emily always moves in the bath; I'll just have a bath and then I'll know she's OK.' I lay there prodding, poking and tapping my tummy but she didn't seem to respond. 'I can feel my tummy hardening though,' I said to Tim. Still concerned, we thought about contacting the midwife. I felt I was worrying over nothing, after all: 'God wouldn't let anything happen, would he?'

Yet I knew that was no reason not to seek the professional advice he had provided. I phoned my mother first.

As I was on the phone, I felt my first painful contraction; it was mild, but the tightening had brought a definite pain with it this time: a sharp stab across the bottom of my womb. Then I phoned the doctor.

'I don't think I've felt baby move. Could the doctor just check her, for my peace of mind, please?'

As I put Abigail in the car, I thought: 'This is silly, a waste of time, I just felt her move anyway.' I had felt my womb tighten and bulge under my ribs.

The traffic was bad and I had to be there in ten minutes. I took a shortcut, but that way was worse. I did a five-point turn in a small space and began again.

'I just want to go home!' Abigail wailed.

'So does Mummy,' I said, through tears. I was frust-rated at being so late and still felt it was a waste of time.

Half an hour later, I knocked at the paned-glass door of the surgery. It was out of hours now and the Saturday morning clinic had ended. The doctor was waiting; he led us through the empty waiting area, to his room. I lay down on the couch. He moved his Sonicaid (a handheld device which enables the foetal heart to be heard with ultrasound vibrations) around and tried various places, but couldn't find a heartbeat.

'He's not my antenatal doctor,' I thought. 'He's just not checking in the right place.' Still unable to find a heart-beat he sent me to the labour ward so they could check.

'We just need to go to the hospital so they can check Mummy's tummy, and then we'll go home and have lunch,' I said to Abigail and I didn't believe for one second that this would not be the case. I didn't even tell Tim we were going.

We waited in a small, seated area at the end of the labour ward. I was not worried. I felt a fraud for being there and even more so as the midwife led me into a little delivery room. She examined my tummy and listened for the 'bumpety, bumpety, bumpety' of Emily's heart. Abigail and I had listened to it so often; in fact only four days ago at my antenatal appointment, we had heard it clearly. Yet this midwife could not find a heartbeat either; she could not hear the usual 'swish, swish' of the placenta. She said she couldn't even tell which position the baby was in. At this, I did feel slightly more worried.

'We need to get the doctor to scan you,' she said.

'Oh, well, that's OK then, the scan will show it up,' I thought. I was told it might take a while, so I phoned Tim. Miraculously he was by the phone and not outside still working on the car. He loves working on cars and spends what time he can in the garage, fixing and rebuilding whatever sporty classic we can find cheap enough to buy. This morning he had been changing the brake pads on Fred's car and had just finished when the phone rang.

'Hi, it's me,' I said, 'they can't find a heartbeat.'

'Oh, no!'

'I'm sure it's OK,' I reassured him. 'They just need to do a scan. Can you come?'

As I waited for Tim the minutes just wouldn't pass; I kept looking at the clock only to find that time had not moved on. The room was small and bare. I was sitting on a short, narrow bed; a long curtain stretched the length of the room behind me and a gap revealed gas and air, linen, towels and bowls, but most prominent was the newborn cot and blankets.

The midwives kept popping in and offering me cups of tea, but I felt sick; every mild contraction brought with it a wave of nausea. My eyes watched the door, waiting for Tim. Someone passed and placed my medical notes on the other side of the door. Suddenly I felt trapped; they were admitting me.

'Why?' I wondered, 'I was only here for a quick check, my contractions weren't even strong enough for me to be in yet.'

Tim arrived. I felt instant relief as I saw his strong, lean figure enter the room. I looked at his handsome face, his dark hair and brown eyes; narrow rimmed glasses that sat on his sharp nose which matched his angular chin. In his face all I saw was concern for me. He took charge and phoned Rachel to collect Abigail. Rachel was another friend from church. Rachel, Steve and their three children live just a few roads away from us. They were on 'labour standby' to look after Abigail. Rachel and I would try to meet once a week to pray together about whatever was on our minds. We did this, grabbing quick moments between watching what Jacob, her three year old son, and Abigail, were up to. One day I had got home to find Abigail was leaving a trail of clumps of blonde hair behind her; not white blonde like Jacob's, but her own darker shade.

'Oh no Abigail, what have you done to your hair?' I asked.

'Scissors!' she replied.

'You cut your hair,' I said.

'Jacob did it,' she replied. I didn't think he had done, he said he hadn't and then I remembered all the times Abigail had watched me trim my own hair in front of the bathroom mirror.

'Oh no, she's been copying me,' I thought and I knew she had done it and that she had blamed Jacob! It was getting well past lunchtime now and Abigail's patience was only extended by the prospect of going to Jacob's house for lunch.

I met Rachel in the corridor. She hugged me, tears in her eyes.

'It's all right,' I said, 'they're just going to check everything on the scan. We'll come and pick Abigail up soon.'

As we sat and waited in that tiny room, I thought of all the Bible verses I had read in recent weeks as I had prayed through my anxieties about giving birth. I felt confident everything was going to be OK.

The doctor poked and prodded for some time, using copious amounts of gel.

'We need a more detailed scan and someone with more expertise,' he said.

As he left the room to make those arrangements the midwife sat on the bed and, looking directly at me, uttered, 'It doesn't look good, I'm afraid.'

Shocked, I leaned against Tim's chest and sobbed.

We sat and cried for a while, then we prayed. What we prayed I don't really remember; I suppose we prayed that everything would be fine, that Emily would be OK and that God would help us in our situation – whatever that was.

'I just don't believe it, do you?'

We still had hope; they needed to do another scan. We phoned our parents and more people began to pray.

'I just want to go home,' I told Tim. 'I should never have bothered the GP, it's such a waste of Saturday and everything will be fine anyway.'

As the hours went slowly by, I still could not eat or drink. I had an upset stomach, worsening nausea and stronger contractions. I sat on the bed with the ultrasound machine on my right and the phone trolley on my left. I felt so ill. Yet I was so fearful and afraid that I couldn't let myself be sick.

As we waited, the possibility of death gradually dawned on us. The sadness I felt was for Abigail.

'It must be a very brave person who would have another baby after this,' I said to Tim. 'It looks like Abigail will be an only child now, doesn't it?'

'Maybe, maybe not,' Tim replied.

'Oh, I don't think I could ever go through another pregnancy,' I responded. I am not one of those people who enjoy being pregnant; not one of those people who find they feel at their best when expecting. Rather, I feel sick and 'grotty' for the first four and even six months and continually exhausted throughout. That mid-trimester 'glow' had never happened to me. With Emily I had also felt quite depressed. Tim and I had decided that unless God seemed to show us otherwise, we would prefer not to have any more children after Emily. We had always wanted more than one and had become quite settled on two. Children themselves are difficult and tiring. Pregnancy had been a continual strain on my energy and my patience. Now, it looked like the cost of bringing up more than one was just too high.

Tim seemed more able to take a step back and look at life on a wider scale at this point, whereas I felt that the response I was feeling now would last for ever. I called the midwife and told her that if Emily had died I wanted a caesarean under general anaesthetic. I could not go through labour, I just wanted to wake up and it all be over.

'That's not our policy,' she informed us, 'there are too many risks for you to go under a general anaesthetic when there's no reason.'

'No reason!' I thought. 'What about all the emotional trauma?'

'You can have a pain-free labour, with an epidural,' she continued.

That was no consolation; it had been my intention all along, especially following the unbelievable pain of the contractions with my first child.

Half an hour before our next scan, we walked around the car park for some fresh air. It was dark now and cold too. We looked down across the city. All the lights were on, sparkling in the distance. I turned to Tim.

'I think we know, don't we?'

'Yes, they certainly haven't been in any hurry, have they?'

I remembered the story of Jesus and Jairus's daughter: 'When he arrived at the house of Jairus, he did not let anyone go in with him, except Peter, John and James, and the child's father and mother. Meanwhile, all the people were wailing and mourning for her. "Stop wailing," Jesus said. "She is not dead but asleep."[1] 'They laughed at him, knowing that she was dead. But he took her by the hand and said, "My child, get up!" Her spirit returned, and at once she stood up.'[2]

'God has the power to raise the dead,' I thought, and I knew that he could make Emily live; he was in control.

We returned to the ward; the consultant radiologist had arrived. I lay on the bed and waited. The midwife, radiologist and obstetrician all came in and the scan began. They turned the screen towards me. I didn't know whether to look or not. I didn't want to discover she was dead myself, so I looked away.

It didn't take long. The radiologist shook his head.

'I'm so sorry,' he said. Tim and I cried in each other's arms. My mind filled with these words.

'When you pass through the waters, I will be with you; and when you pass through the rivers, they will not sweep over you.'[3]

That was one of those verses I had read in the Bible when I'd prayed about Emily's birth. I'd had such a bad time

giving birth to Abigail that as I'd waited for Emily I'd needed a lot of reassurance. I remember thinking at the time that
this verse was a little bit odd. It didn't imply, as I would
have liked, that I was necessarily in for a smooth ride.

'Oh well,' I had thought, 'at least I'll be able to cope
even though I'm scared.' And I had felt at peace with that.

I look back now, quite amazed and think, 'God never
lies.' He didn't pacify me and say that everything would
be OK, although that was perhaps the way I had chosen
to think. He had said just enough not to worry me at the
time, but to plant in me his words to get me through what
only he knew would happen.

Now, although sad and shocked, I was at peace. I asked
Tim if he was OK, and I too, was able to say, with convic-
tion, 'I'm OK.'

We had been told that Emily hadn't been dead long.
From the scan it looked as though she had died within the
last twenty-four hours. Through tears we made the necessary phone calls.

'Mummy, Emily's in heaven,' I said. I hoped that was
true; I had never really thought a great deal about babies
and heaven. I only presumed they went there on the basis
that God is just and babies are innocent.

'Oh no, I don't believe it.' Words were cut short on the
phone. Sobbing took over each conversation; disbelief
and bewilderment echoed down the lines.

We had been given a choice about what we wanted to
do next. They could induce me now and get everything
going quickly or I could go home and come back when
labour had really got itself going.

Tim and I certainly wanted things dealt with as
quickly as possible and I knew that it wouldn't be long
before I would have to be in the hospital for pain relief
anyway. Yet we were keen to see Abigail and tell her what

happened; we didn't want her to expect us to return with a baby. I also needed some space. I felt trapped; I just wanted to be in my own house.

We decided to go home for a few hours, see Abigail and gather our things and ourselves together for what lay ahead.

It was with heavy hearts that we left the hospital, passing other newborns with big bright helium balloons attached to their car-seats: 'It's a girl!', 'Congratulations', 'A New Baby'.

2

ABIGAIL

Abigail, my sweet darling Abigail, with her clear blue eyes and blonde bobbed hair. I was envious of her hair, so straight and neat, while mine had always been a clump of frizzy curls. She was so young, understood everything, even the smallest thing did not escape her notice and nothing was ever forgotten. For seven months, we had worked very hard to prepare her for the baby's arrival. She had been involved in all my antenatal checks and she had helped paint Emily's room. She did this with her own little sponge roller. Then bored with that, she would put her hands flat in the paint and print them all over the walls. She didn't seem to mind that I went over them with my roller. Together we had quickly turned the dull blue into bright yellow. We had bought all Emily's baby things together too; nappies, bottles and dummies. Abigail had gone through her toys and chosen the ones to pass on to Emily, although she would often go into Emily's room and play with them.

'Emily is sharing them with me,' she said.

Sometimes Abigail would come and hug my tummy, saying, 'I'm giving Emily a cuddle.' She would put her hands on my tummy and feel her move. With pride she told others: 'I'm going to be a sister.' I was delighted in how involved she was in the pregnancy.

After all this my biggest concern was how we were going to tell Abigail that Emily had died. How would she cope with such a disappointment? Dad had reassured me that young children bounce back and get over things quickly. This gave me the confidence to tackle the task.

We collected Abigail and asked her, 'How would you like to sleep at Jacob's house tonight?' Her excitement could hardly be contained, so we went home to pack an overnight bag.

At home we all sat down on the sofa.

'We need to tell you something sad,' we began. 'Abigail . . . '

'Yes?'

'Emily has gone to heaven, so we're not going to have her here after all.' I looked into her young face. It was unlined by life's troubles.

'Mummy has still got to go into hospital though, to get sorted out, but she won't be bringing Emily back.'

'Owh.' The little blank face, looked from one of us to the other as she took in our tears.

We continued to explain that Emily had gone, until we were sure she understood. Normally when there was a change of plan we could find something else to do or something to have instead, but there was nothing we could replace Emily with. Nothing to ease the pain. No promise of 'But she'll come another day.'

Abigail did however cope very well. She knew all about heaven already. Her favourite Bible story had, for some time, been Jesus' ascension into heaven. She would colour in a glittery Jesus going up into the clouds. She had been taught that heaven was a nice place, where people were happy and where Jesus had a place waiting for you. She was able to accept that this was where Emily had gone. While we all cried together, she went and got the tissues.

'I cuddle you and make you happy,' she said when she returned, her plump hands clutching wads of Kleenex. Then she continued to busy herself with packing, looking forward to her exciting night away from home.

With Abigail taken care of, I began to think of our return to hospital. We too needed to get our things together. Instead of taking Emily's previously packed bag, we sombrely chose one sleepsuit we both liked. I wanted to take them all, but there wasn't much point as she could only wear one. We took a favourite towel and a cuddly rabbit that had been waiting for her. This rabbit was my favourite. It had been mine before we had children.

It was the midwives at the hospital who had suggested we bring Emily some things. We had no idea about anything in these situations; it wasn't something we had contemplated, not even for a second. They helped to lead us through what to do, what was needed, what we had to think about and decide upon. We were grateful for this, as our plans had been well laid, over months, for Emily's birth and homecoming. Now we had to swing right round to prepare to receive her dead instead of alive and consider her funeral, all in a very short space of time, when it was hard to think straight.

The fear of going through labour only to give birth to a dead child was like a worst nightmare come true. I sat in our bathroom; I needed the toilet constantly. Tim popped his head round the door, every so often.

'I'm not ready yet, I'll be down in a minute.' I wanted to be by myself. I was shaking all over. My legs trembling so violently, I could hardly keep my feet on the floor. I hadn't eaten or drunk anything all day. I was trying very hard to drink a few mouthfuls of sugary apple squash; I had eaten half a rich tea biscuit; but now I could swallow nothing else. I was terrified of being sick.

'If I'm sick now, I will never stop.' I thought irrationally. I was light-headed and leant my head against the cold bathroom wall. My forearms were going numb and tingly. I was trying to get on top of my panic, trying to distract myself; but the situation I was in offered little distraction.

'I could just stay here a little longer. Oh, if only I could stay here for ever, in my own bathroom, in my own house and not have to leave to go to the hospital, to . . .' I could not form the thoughts of what lay ahead, it was too terrible even to think about. I looked down at the fluffy cream bath mat, with its bright yellow flowers, at my feet, looked around at all our familiar things and thought I would never have the courage to get up.

'I cannot do this, I can't go through with this.' But I knew I had no choice. Emily had to come out, but still I battled, forcing myself to move. I remembered the suffering of Jesus, how he had cried out, to be spared the agony of the cross, 'My soul is overwhelmed with sorrow to the point of death'.[4]

'He . . . knelt down and prayed, "Father, if you are willing, take this cup from me; yet not my will, but yours be done." An angel from heaven appeared to him and strengthened him. And being in anguish, he prayed more earnestly, and his sweat was like drops of blood falling to the ground.'[5] I thought on how he understood pain. I knew that he was with me and would get me through it. I thought that the sooner I got to the hospital, the sooner I would get some pain relief, something to ease my nausea and the sooner it would all be over. Steve would be here in a minute, to give us a lift to the hospital.

'I'd better get downstairs.' Shakily and with much hesitation I finally made it out of the front door.

3

EMILY

We were taken to a large, beautiful room, tastefully decorated with its bright curtains and pictures, more like a hotel than a hospital. At one end there was a comfortable high-backed carver chair and matching rocking chair, placed either side of a coffee table. On top of this there were magazines and flowers. The sleeping area had an extra bed, which had been brought in for Tim. They apologised for the room! It was not the special suite that was usually offered in these circumstances; that was already occupied.

'I'm sorry there's no telly and the bathroom is down the other end of the corridor,' the midwife said sympathetically.

'Oh, that's OK,' we replied.

'We can't deliver you in here, not with an epidural, as there's no oxygen supply.'

'Oh, OK,' I said, but I thought. 'Oxygen. Why would I need oxygen? I hadn't had it before. Oh no. Am I going to die too?' I pulled myself together sharply. 'Don't be so ridiculous!' I said to myself. 'Don't you remember the promise you felt God made you, as you contemplated marriage?'

'For the Lord is your life, and he will give you many years . . .'[6]

'Oh yes,' I thought, 'I won't worry then.'

We settled down; Tim left me the rocking chair, but I preferred the carver; the motion to and fro was not helping my stomach. We waited for someone to come and induce me.

We sat there and talked and tried to read a little. I was feeling more ill with each contraction and I thought, 'Here we are, everyone else coming in to have their baby to take home and we'll have nothing.' We decided to read the Bible and pray for a bit, I so needed to hear what God was going to say about all this.

Our Bible reading notes turned us to the first chapter of Daniel. Here Daniel, a prophet of God, and three other young men from Judah were among those called into service for King Nebuchadnezzar. These men refused to eat the royal food and wine because it had been offered to idols; instead they only had vegetables and water. As we read the account one verse stood out among the rest: 'At the end of the ten days they looked healthier and better nourished than any of the young men who ate the royal food.'[7] It seemed that God was saying to us, 'It might look like you're missing out on the good things that everyone else has, but I will make you even better off for it.' What reassurance, what peace and how clear the words of God were as they brought comfort into our moment of sadness and anxiety.

Tim was keen to see his parents and we invited them to come and be with us for a while. This was particularly special as their third child had also been stillborn at the end of the pregnancy. Just knowing that they knew what we were going through was a great comfort. They came and shared our tears. They moved the extra bed over to the chairs, so that we could all sit comfortably together. They talked about their trip to Salisbury, earlier in the day. Having them there brought some normality and a feeling of stability in this very foreign and terrifying situation.

I was induced and given an injection of pethidine and phenytoin for the pain and nausea; then I was encouraged to get some sleep. Tim's parents left promising to return with their little pocket 'telly'. I needed some distraction. It gave a fuzzy picture, but at midnight on a Saturday evening there was very little to watch. Tim fell asleep quickly in the bed beside me, but I never slept. The pethidine made me feel relaxed and drowsy and took the edge off the pain for a little while. I still vomited despite the anti-sickness drug. I lay there in a dozy state feeling that this wasn't quite as horrific as I'd imagined.

I worried about seeing my dead baby.

'What would she look like? Would I like her like that?' – the midwife had explained to me that if the baby had been dead some time then I was to expect some blistered and peeling skin.

'Will you have a look first and check, so that I'm prepared?' I asked.

'Yes, of course,' she promised. I leant back into the pillows.

I felt a fraud; taking up the bed in this beautiful birthing room. Here I was, on a labour ward being cared for by midwives and I wasn't even having a child, not a real one; well, at least not a live one anyway. I felt more justified in thinking that we were ill. That I had to be here because I would get very ill if she didn't come out!

As labour progressed I was in increasingly more pain. When I first asked for my epidural, labour was not sufficiently established. I tried to make do with painkillers and a sleeping pill. I was able to relax again, although not sleep properly. I lay there, drifting in and out of slumber, coming to with the noise of an extractor fan flapping in the wind and cries of pain drifting up the corridor. I counted slowly to twenty as each contraction gripped me and when I could bear it no longer I called again for my epidural. This time I was ready. I was pushed in a wheelchair to the delivery room.

'The anaesthetist will be about twenty minutes, she's with someone else at the moment. More pethidine?'

'Yes and I feel sick.'

'I'm afraid there's nothing more I can give you for that, you're just one of those people who are sick in labour. These contractions are coming thick and fast, there's a chance you won't get the epidural in time.'

My controlled breathing had become deep groans of agony; I began weeping through each contraction. I pushed Tim out of my way as he tried to help.

'I can't go on without an epidural,' I cried. There were now only a few seconds between each anguishing grip.

'I'll try and hurry things along, do you feel ready to push?'

'No,' I needed that epidural now. 'Oh God, help me!'

The anaesthetist arrived and began to prepare me for my spinal block.

'This is going to feel cold,' she said.

'Yes, yes,' I thought. 'Get on with it.' A freezing spray covered my back and made me jump.

'I'm pushing!' I shouted. I was still sitting upright on the edge of the bed, pushing down into it. They moved me round to lie against the back of the bed.

'Push!' they said. As I did so I screamed and screamed.

'Pant. Pant . . . Push.' My screaming, louder and louder, turned into high-pitched shrieks. I could see myself lying there. I looked at my face, screwed up in agony. I was gagging with the pain.

Another midwife rushed in. Her face in mine, she tried to calm me down. I looked into her eyes. I noticed how their sparkle had faded with the long night hours. The fresh mascara was now hidden by dark circles. I could take no notice of her pleading to stop my hysteria. My loud cries were more than pain, they were a vent for my grief, a release for my sorrow and even the start of my healing.

'It's over, it's over,' the relief was immense as Emily's body left mine. I looked at her lying there and into the sad faces at the foot of the bed.

'She's beautiful,' I said quietly. They wrapped her in a towel and handed her to me. She felt wonderful; a warm little bundle of baby. Seemingly asleep, she lay in my arms. Yet not moving; not making a sound. I looked at every part of her and examined all her fingers and toes. She was small, weighing five pounds, one ounce. She was absolutely perfectly formed, with just a little blister developing on the top of her arm. Her dark crimson lips and nails were a stark reminder that she was indeed dead. A mass of dark wavy hair crowned her head. I know all young babies have blue eyes, but I had to check. I had to see all of Emily. I needed to know her. I gently lifted her eyelid. Her pupil was small and contracted, the centre of a rich blue iris.

The midwife carefully helped me bathe Emily. I lovingly wiped around her ears with wet cotton wool. When I was satisfied she was clean I lifted her into her own towel. The midwife left. Tim and I dressed Emily together, putting her in the sleepsuit we had chosen. We wept continually. We took it in turns to cuddle and hold Emily, as we each took photos. We prayed together, thanking God for Emily and committing her to him. When we felt we could do no more for her, we laid her in a Moses basket and we all returned to our room. We sat looking at her lovingly and took more photos. When we had finished she was taken into the room next door; close by, just in case we wanted to see her again.

There were, again, many phone calls to make. This time, to say that it was all over. Stunned silence continued to prevail as we spoke to our relatives.

'She was beautiful you know,' I tried to fill the quiet.

We knew that Tim's mum had not been given the choice of seeing her own stillborn child. We wanted to give her the opportunity of seeing ours. A little later, she entered the room, tears in her eyes. I treasure the moment she lifted Emily out of the cot, talking to her, telling her how lovely she was; just as she would have, if she had been alive.

We phoned my parents and invited them to come and see Emily too. They had a long way to travel from Poole. As we waited for them to arrive, we tried to eat and drink a little and I wanted a bath.

The thought of being alone, even for a second, frightened me, so Tim sat with me while I bathed. I began to feel sick again. I could not bear to look at my body; it was not just that it was saggy and misshapen from the pregnancy, but it was a failure, a body that could not keep its own child alive. Tim helped me to step out of the bath, I was light-headed from the pethidine.

Back in our room, I sat resting on the bed, thoughts flooding my mind. I thought, 'How can I be absolutely sure Emily is in heaven? That she is OK?' Again, I had the pressing desire to hear what God had to say. I asked Tim to pass me the Bible. As I flicked through the Psalms, my eye caught this verse, 'How lovely is your dwelling-place, O Lord Almighty!' And as if that wasn't enough, I turned the page. My body shook with great sobs; Tim came rushing to me, but I was crying with immense relief and even joy. The words read:

My soul yearns, even faints, for the courts of the Lord; my heart and my flesh cry out for the living God.

Even the sparrow has found a home, and the swallow a nest for herself, where she may have her young – a place near your altar,

O Lord Almighty, my King and my God. Blessed are those who dwell in your house; they are ever praising you.

Blessed are those whose strength is in you, who have set their hearts on pilgrimage. As they pass through the Valley of Baca, they make it a place of springs; the autumn rains also cover it with pools. They go from strength to strength, till each appears before God in Zion. Hear my prayer, O Lord God Almighty; listen to me, O God of Jacob. Look upon our shield, O God; look with favour on your anointed one.

Better is one day in your courts than a thousand elsewhere; I would rather be a doorkeeper in the house of my God than dwell in the tents of the wicked.

For the Lord God is a sun and shield; the Lord bestows favour and honour; no good thing does he withhold from those whose walk is blameless.

O Lord Almighty, blessed is the man who trusts in you.[8]

Emily had gone to a far better place; she is where we all long to be. She is more than happy, she is blessed. Is she missing out on life? No. One day in heaven is better than a thousand on earth! God is not withholding anything good from her, for her walk was blameless; she did not get the chance to do anything wrong. As I trusted in these words, I knew that God had spoken, clearer than I had ever experienced before. I was truly comforted and at peace.

The midwife came in with a young, awkward-looking doctor; we were given Emily's death certificate and papers for the funeral director. We had decided to make our own

funeral arrangements. The doctor silently handed us a
postmortem consent form.

'This is probably the first time she's had to do this,' I
thought. We read and signed what we felt we wanted
done. I just followed Tim's lead; agreeing with what he
said, trusting his judgement. It was all too much to take
in. I wasn't terribly bothered about the 'nitty-gritty' of it
all. Since she was dead already, I was quite happy for
them to do what they needed to, to find out why she had
died. So I just signed where Tim indicated. We were also
given a pile of leaflets containing various help lines.

Tim was keen to get home. I was a little more reluctant.
I wondered how things would be, once we left the
cocooned hospital ward and returned to the real world.

My parents arrived at one o'clock. It was not quite the
original plan for Emily's birth. They were going to come
and stay to look after Abigail when I went into labour. Now,
the thought of them coming to stay was more than I could
cope with. It would be too painful. I had been so looking
forward to their stay. I had imagined Mum helping me with
Emily and keeping the house in order and the meals
cooked. Now things were so different. To have gone ahead
as planned would have been a very poor compensation.
Mum and Dad decided to book into a 'bed and breakfast'
instead. They would be around when we needed them.

There was a soft knock on the door. I opened it and
there they were. They looked awful. My mum was a frag-
ment of her usual self. She looked lost and sad, weak and
vulnerable. They had travelled a long way in bad traffic
but were so pleased to be with us.

'Oh, you both look so much better than we thought,'
Dad remarked with relief.

'You're being so brave,' Mum said. I didn't feel brave. I
was finding it extremely difficult to see them so sad. I had

to try to cope with their grief as well as my own. I wanted to comfort them but they just wanted to comfort us. I felt so sorry that I was not giving them their next grandchild. There would be one missing from the family.

'Do you want to see Emily now?'

'Yes, yes,' they both replied earnestly.

'She won't look as nice now. It's been several hours.' I tried to prepare them for the cold, grey body. They knew more about these things than I did; Mum, after all, had been a nurse and midwife; but I still felt the need to protect them.

I wasn't sure whether I wanted to see Emily again now, or just remember her as she was. My decision was made by my strong desire to be the one to show them Emily. Like any proud mum, I wanted to see what they thought of her. The midwife brought her in and left us to it.

'Oh, she's so lovely,'

'So pretty.'

'Does she look a bit like Abigail?'

'No, no, she's different,' I said in reply to my mother's question. 'Would you like to hold her?'

I picked up her cold, lifeless body and cradled her in my arms once more. This was not the nice warm cuddle I remembered. This wasn't the baby I felt I could keep. I must have looked so pathetic cuddling my dead child. My father who doesn't usually show his emotions, started crying. I carefully handed Emily to my mum. I rushed to hug Dad and offer him some comfort.

'It's OK, Dad, we're all right,' I said.

'Oh don't worry about me, I'm OK,' he replied, emphasising the 'me' and 'I'.

Mum handed Emily to Dad and he cuddled her too. Few words were spoken in these moments, it was deep grief which filled the room; disbelief and dismay. We put

Emily back into her cot. Dad prayed over her, committing her to God, thanking God for her little life. Then we said goodbye, again. Dad's a church minister and it felt nice to have him pray like that. It was an official farewell at the last time of seeing her. She was taken back into the other room and we got ready to leave. It was time to go now, time to leave her behind. As we left the room I had a peek next door. Emily's basket was sitting on a bed next to another Moses basket. I did not enter, but said silently, 'Goodbye Emily,' and I thought, 'we're not leaving her alone, she has a little friend next to her.' That was comforting.

Mum and Dad went to find some lunch and we went to pick up Abigail and have some time to settle down.

'I wish I hadn't seen and held her again,' I said to Tim on the way home, 'she seemed so dead, she was all cold.'

'I know, that's why I didn't hold her again,' Tim replied.

'Perhaps it's best that I did though; maybe it will serve to help me accept she was really dead and not just asleep. Tim, I so loved Emily's warm body when she was born. I so wanted to keep her then. But when I held her just now, there didn't seem to be a great deal of point in hanging on to her.'

All we were taking home were memories; a handprint and footprint, Emily's hospital tags and the promise of some photos from our camera.

4

AT HOME

&c&r&~&

We arrived home and put Abigail down for her afternoon nap. We listened to our answer machine messages. As we picked up the phone to invite Fred and Margaret over we saw them walk up the path. They were carrying with them a tin of freshly baked, home-made biscuits; they know how I love biscuits. As they came in, no one said a word. We hugged and cried together; our tears said it all. As I hugged Margaret I felt the bump of her baby between us. I was conscious that in twelve weeks time she would have her baby. Somehow that didn't matter to me; it didn't make any difference to our friendship. That was their baby and part of them – not mine.

As I thought about it I realised what God had given us was different. Yes, it was sad and it hurt deeply and dreadfully because we could not keep Emily. Yet God had still given us a beautiful baby. Emily had not been a mistake. She was a good gift from God. This is what the Bible says, 'Sons are a heritage from the Lord, children a reward from him.'[9]

She had been planned for this time, by us and by God. He had created her from us and he had given us the privilege of nurturing her, not to live in this life, but so that she could live in heaven.

For whatever reason, Emily's life being so short was in his plan for us and for her and we trusted him. I thought of the Bible verse I knew so well. It was one that a friend had shown me when I was at university. I had been standing in his room one Saturday lunchtime; I was taking a break from the books that crowded my desk in the room next door. Our other housemates were out. I looked out of the window into the street.

'What are you looking for?' he asked.

'A horse.'

'What?'

'A horse; being ridden by a shining knight, coming to whisk me away. Look, there he is!' I pretended to see a gallant man riding down the road. I had been out of a relationship for a little while and was impatient to find my soul mate.

'Aren't you bothered you haven't got a girlfriend?' I asked.

'No,' he replied 'because someone found this for me.' He opened up his Bible and pointed: ' "For I know the plans I have for you," declares the Lord, ' "plans to prosper you and not to harm you, plans to give you hope and a future." '[10] Later I took a green pen and highlighted these words in my own Bible. Now, seven years on, in a different situation, it became a promise to trust in. We were not going to be worse off, not going to be harmed, but we would prosper with hope and a future.

Fred and Margaret stayed a little while; we sat and chatted. I couldn't help but tell Margaret how painful childbirth was. This probably wasn't what she needed to hear, but she listened nonetheless. It felt good to talk about it. My baby wasn't in my arms now, but my experience of her birth was no less than any other mother's.

Tim's mum and sister arrived a little later. They brought flowers and a present for Abigail. I had to fight back the tears when I saw Abigail's present, it should have been for Emily. It was Bagpuss – 'an old saggy cloth cat and *Emily* loved him'. I felt he should at least have been mine. I wanted to cuddle something, but Abigail was so pleased with him that we were never able to become very acquainted.

My parents returned after a little while. They looked so much better and were even smiling. We were all so relieved to have got this far. It had been so nice to share in Emily's memory together. I let them in quietly while Tim continued to give Abigail her tea in the other room. Her excitement at seeing them would have overtaken any thoughts of food.

'Grandma and Granddad!' she exclaimed when she saw them. I still found it strange to hear my parents called that. Nice, but strange.

I had eaten virtually nothing for the last thirty-six hours; I felt like I would never be able to eat again. Now, sitting in the front room, my feet curled up beside me while Tim made tea, I was able to manage three fish fingers and felt quite proud. Exhausted, we went early to bed. We took sleeping pills to help us switch off from the day's events. As I lay in bed, my hands reached to feel my tummy as I had become accustomed to do. I drew them back sharply. I could not touch the wobbly flesh. It was a void; an empty womb, heightening the emptiness of my world. It screamed of the ugly failure of my body.

I awoke at 3 a.m. My hands moved to my tummy again; there was no mound. My eyes looked through the darkness into Emily's room; she was not there either. I thought of the people I needed to tell and I cried from the depth of my heart. Nothing could stop the wrenching sobs.

'I want your mum,' I told Tim as he held me close.

'My mum?' Tim asked.

'Yes, she'll know how I feel.' I felt it should be my mother I wanted, but I needed to see someone who had been through it too. Tim phoned his mum and made me some warm, sugary milk.

We sat on the sofa, in the middle of the night, Barbara's arms around me, my head leaning against her shoulder, my words tumbling out on top of each other, between big gasps for air.

'What was that?' she asked softly.

'I woke up, she wasn't there, not in my tummy, not in her cot, she wasn't there.'

'I know, it comes as such a shock.' Knowing she had experienced my pain I could allow her words to comfort me, like no one else's would. I knew she understood, she didn't just empathise, she could really sympathise.

A little later, I was ready for sleep again. We slept peacefully until Abigail came bounding in at half past seven, with her usual, 'Can I have my breakfast now?'

At the kitchen sink Abigail asked, 'Where's Emily?'

I gasped and looking at her, my eyes swimming with tears, I replied, 'She's in heaven, sweetheart.'

'Jesus is looking after her,' she stated.

'That's right,' I said.

We went back upstairs and got dressed. Tim got up and I got Abigail ready; Mum and Dad were coming at half past nine to take her out for a walk. This meant Tim and I would have some time to ourselves. We had a lot of post to open. The postman had struggled to get all the cards through the door; they had dropped with a great thud and then sprawled out all over the floor.

Abigail was excited about going out, but when my parents knocked on the door suddenly everything must have felt strange and she was reluctant to leave. We encouraged her to go and then Tim and I sat down in a heap on the sofa with a cup of tea. Taking advantage of the quiet we picked up our Bible and accompanying daily reading notes. We prayed that God would speak to us as we read. We were hurting deeply and I was anxious; so many thoughts were washing in and out of my mind, there was barely space to grab one and think it through. I needed someone to tell me everything was all right. Someone that I could trust, someone whose word I could accept needed to be in control – the burden was too heavy for me to bear alone. Our Bible readings continued in Daniel.

In chapter 3 King Nebuchadnezzar set up an image of gold to be worshipped and Shadrach, Meshach and Abednego were thrown into a fiery furnace because they refused to do so. As the king watched he saw something incredible:

> Then King Nebuchadnezzar leaped to his feet in amazement and asked his advisers, 'Weren't there three men that we tied up and threw into the fire?'
>
> They replied, 'Certainly, O king.'
>
> He said, 'Look! I see four men walking around in the fire, unbound and unharmed, and the fourth looks like the son of the gods.'[11]

God had been there with those men, right in the heat of the flames, he protected them and they came out unharmed: 'the fire had not harmed their bodies, nor was a hair of their heads singed; their robes were not scorched, and there was no smell of fire on them.'[12] Even though the furnace was so hot that it had killed the soldiers who had put the men in!

As we read this we knew that God was with us too, right in the middle of our grief and we were confident we would be unharmed as well.

When Nebuchadnezzar had threatened the three men this is what they had said, 'If we are thrown into the blazing furnace, the God we serve is able to save us from it, and he will rescue us from your hand, O king. But even if he does not, we want you to know, O king, that we will not serve your gods or worship the image of gold you have set up.'[13]

As our Bible notes explained, God could have saved the men. And indeed he did, but even if he had not it would have made no difference to them. God was bigger than their circumstance. This made me think of Emily; God could have saved her for this life, could have even brought her back from the dead, but he did not, and this was making no difference to our faith, because God was bigger than this circumstance. He was indeed in control. He had a better life planned for Emily in heaven.

We felt so encouraged, God was with us, he was in control and he wasn't going to let us be harmed. Now we could face the day.

I phoned my friends at work and told them what had happened. They came to see me at lunchtime, bringing flowers, a teddy for Abigail and offering much sympathy. I was grateful; it felt good to be cared for by so many people. Martin, our church minister, popped in mid-morning and prayed with us. Strangely, just like Fred and Margaret, he had come just as we were about to phone and ask him to. Martin is a young man in his mid-thirties. He and his wife have three children, all boys. Like many of our friends they were praying for us and shared deeply in our sadness. Now Martin prayed with us, for God's help through our grief.

The midwife also came that morning, checked me over physically and we talked for a while as she offered me her deepest sympathy.

My parents returned bringing fresh bread for lunch, bubble bath for me and chocolate for Tim. Abigail was carrying a magazine with glittery pens hanging off the front, by a now single piece of twisted Sellotape. She had an enormous grin on her face, having had enjoyed her morning after all.

Halfway through lunch there was a knock on the door and there stood our GP. I invited him into the front room and went through what had happened. I was getting used to telling people – it also helped me to get it straight in my head. Our doctor was very reassuring too. I stored up in my mind what he said, 'If ever you need antide-pressants, don't feel you've failed. Depression is an ill-ness like any other.'

It was true, I was likely to see these drugs as a failure; they still carry a big stigma. So although I didn't need them at that point, I later pondered his comments and felt I came to understand a little more about God's healing. I believe God can heal, directly if he chooses to; the Bible is full of God's miracles. Jesus healed the sick, as did his disciples after him. However, more often it would seem, he guides us to the doctor. All knowledge and wisdom comes from God and he has given humanity medical knowledge. I believe it would be irresponsible not to use it. Indeed, when the Bible talks about praying for the sick to be healed, it talks about anointing with oil, and as well as a symbol of the Holy Spirit, oil was one of the best known ancient medicines.

'Is any one of you sick? He should call the elders of the church to pray over him and anoint him with oil in the name of the Lord. And the prayer offered in faith will make the sick person well; the Lord will raise him up.'[14]

Although our trust and dependence is to be in God, *'in the name of the Lord'*, *'the prayer offered in faith'*, we should still use medicine.

We finished what was a surprisingly happy lunch and we put our exhausted Abigail to bed. Mum and Dad sat down to rest and shooed us out. We had decided it would be good to get out of the house and we drove the short drive to the supermarket. According to Tim and my parents I was apparently still too weak to walk, although I had felt I would manage.

We dawdled around the aisles. So much food, so much choice, so many tasty things to eat, now what did I fancy? Nothing. I could have chosen anything, but there was nothing that grabbed me, nothing that I wanted in the whole shop. Tim, nevertheless, picked up five jam doughnuts to have with our afternoon tea. It did feel good to be out, to be somewhere normal, but still I could not forget for a second what had happened. As I looked around it felt so strange. I looked at those who knew nothing of what I had been through, those who made no allowances when I stood in the way, absorbed in my own little world, or bumped into their trolley. I pulled Tim's arm.

'Look,' I said and he lifted his head in the direction I had nodded in. There was someone we knew, someone we needed to tell, but not here, not now. Afraid that we would be spotted we hurried towards the other end of the shop, we kept an eye on his movements and dodged in between the aisles keeping out of sight. Tim had the energy to wander around for a while, but I began to feel faint.

'I'm only walking slowly around a shop,' I thought, 'and I'm so exhausted.' With no crying baby, it was easy to forget I'd just given birth.

'I'm too tired now,' I said to Tim, 'good job we didn't walk.' He smiled knowingly and we returned home.

Abigail was still asleep, Mum and Dad were reading. I flopped down beside them, glad to be home and glad now of the doughnuts. While we had been out several visitors had come with cards, flowers and more bubble bath. So many people showed they cared. We knew they did, but to really feel their love and support was very special.

Later I opened the freezer, wondering what to get everyone for tea. The freezer was packed to the doors with convenience food. I had anticipated being so busy with the new baby that there would be no time to cook. As I looked at the packets everything needed hours to defrost, then another hour of cooking time.

'Oh dear, not so convenient after all.' I took out the large chicken casserole to defrost in the microwave. It wouldn't even fit in.

'Tim,' I called. 'What shall I do?' He took it out of its tray and put it into a smaller dish. Then every few minutes I returned to scrape off the softened edges so that it would fit a little better.

'It's ready,' I called a good hour and a half later, then caught my breath as pain gripped me. It was deep inside my womb and it was not fading like a contraction. Dad came into the kitchen and saw me trying to control my breathing as I hung over the cooker.

'An after-pain,' he thought. 'It will go in a minute,' he said.

'Mmm,' I replied, still waiting for it to ease. A few minutes later it was gone, but still I thought, puzzled, 'These pains aren't like they were after Abigail was born.'

Dinner smelt lovely and it tasted good, but my appetite was poor.

'Abigail, it's time for your bath,' I said and we climbed the stairs hand in hand.

'Can I have Emily's bubbles?' she asked. We had bought Emily some special baby bubble bath when we had been shopping. Abigail had borrowed them a few times, attracted by the elephant picture on the front.

'Yes, you can,' I said to Abigail, 'Emily doesn't need them now, does she?' I took the opportunity to reinforce that Emily would not return. My mum was quiet; tears in her eyes.

'It's OK, Mum,' I said.

'Yes, but sometimes it seems just too sad,' she replied. I nodded.

Later I had a bath.

'Come with me,' I said to Tim. I still could not be alone, so he sat on the edge of the toilet and read a magazine, or tried to, while I lay back and discussed the day.

'Are you sure it's not anything I've done?' I asked. My head buzzed with questions. Had my baths been too hot? Did I overexert myself or did I sleep too much? Should I have noticed something was wrong earlier? Should the midwives have noticed? What about the doctor? It would have been easy to feel guilty or try to apportion blame. The last thing I wanted was to feel resentment on top of my guilt.

'Debs, you know what God has been saying,' Tim replied, 'God is in control, he allowed this to happen and nothing you could have done could have changed it.'

'I know, but still,' I added, 'it's hard to get your head round.'

'Yes, but Emily's life was precious to God; he created her. He would not have let anyone or anything interfere with his plan for her life.'

We slept well that night; I did not wake until the morning. Tim slept on a little while I got up with Abigail. That was unusual, it was so unlike me to be the first up. Yet now I could not lie in bed once I had woken up, as my mind would wander and fill with painful memories. Once I was up these were less intrusive.

At breakfast Abigail sat telling me about her night at Jacob's house, the night that I'd had Emily.

'Jacob wears black pants,' she told me seriously.

'Does he?' I tried to keep a straight face.

'Yes, and I've got pink ones.' Then she climbed on to my knee and in the same breath asked, 'Where's Emily?'

'She's in heaven so we won't be seeing her,' I replied.

'She'll come another day?'

'No, she won't, sweetheart, she's not coming.'

'Owh,' she replied sadly. I comforted her and reassured her Emily was fine, then we set about getting on with the day.

The day took on much the same pattern as the previous one. Mum and Dad took Abigail out in the morning and Tim and I sat down on the sofa and read the Bible. We hugged and cried and we eagerly opened yet another pile of cards.

The words of the Bible again strengthened and comforted us. It also prepared us for the choices we needed to make about Emily's funeral. Still in the book of Daniel these things caught my attention. The theme of idols running through chapter 3 caused me to think about what idols there might be in my life, things that would shift my focus from God, things that would begin to take over my time, my thoughts and my energy in a way that would be unhealthy. Again, I thought of Emily and I felt warned not to turn her into something she wasn't, not to make her grave a shrine.

We read the story of Nebuchadnezzar's dream of a tree, which was interpreted by Daniel. Nebuchadnezzar was like a beautiful, flourishing tree which was going to be cut down, but a stump would remain symbolising he would be restored. Indeed, he became even greater than before. This made us think again that God was not only going to restore us and get us through this, but he had even better things planned. We were filled with excitement. I couldn't believe I was so full of hope, peace and even joy at such a time of tragedy. I wasn't taking any medication but I felt so high I couldn't understand it, not until sometime later I read, 'a crown of beauty instead of ashes, the oil of gladness instead of mourning, and a garment of praise instead of a spirit of despair.'[15]

'Wow,' I thought, 'and this is what God has done for us.'

We wrote a list of all the arrangements we needed to make, all the people we needed to phone and all the things we needed to do. The list was long and daunting. We'd start tomorrow.

As Mum and I cleared up lunch we talked about Emily. We stood by the kitchen sink letting our tears flow. I told Mum about Abigail's breakfast comments and how pleased I was that she was expressing her grief and seemed to understand and accept more readily than any of us what had happened.

After lunch Tim and I went out and into town. We wandered in and out of the shops. I watched everyone else rushing around, agitated and stressed.

'What's the hurry?' I thought. 'Why are you rushing? Nothing can be that important, you can't make your life longer, you can try everything, but when your time's up, it's up.' With that philosophy, nothing seemed to matter very much. In fact it was nice to feel a little more relaxed; I could go home and the dusty furniture didn't shout 'clean me' quite so loudly!

It was raining and we spied an empty table by the window in a coffee shop.

'Let's go in,' Tim suggested.

'OK,' I replied quite happily. I enjoyed my pot of tea as we sat quietly, relaxing together. I took the time to reflect on all that had happened and mulled it over with Tim. Suddenly we realised we were running out of time on the car park ticket so we hurried back. As I walked towards the car another wrenching pain gripped my womb. I slowed down and took in deep breaths of air.

'These after-pains are very bad,' I thought as I waited for them to pass. We drove home and decided what to do that evening. Tim had previously arranged to go to a friend's stag night that evening. He felt up to it so I encouraged him to go. It would do him good to get out with other friends.

After our evening meal, Tim and I went upstairs. Mum and Dad had got the photos of Emily developed for us that morning and I wanted to have a look. Tim had opened the sealed packet and flicked through.

'You might not want to see them,' he said.

'Why not?' I asked. 'I've been so looking forward to them.' Then, as Tim flicked through them while I watched, my heart sank. I was so disappointed.

'That's not Emily,' I said. 'She didn't look like that, these make her look all grey.' This was all I had left of what Emily was like and I couldn't even have that! I felt cheated. I had been looking forward to seeing Emily again, yet the photos were an insufficient substitute. They were an insult to our precious moments when we saw and held her; that time could never be brought back. It was so unfair. Then I remembered that it was important not to make anything an idol, so I accepted them just as photos. It was several weeks before I had the courage to look at them properly and when I did I was very pleased with them. I wept over them for ages as they served to freshen my memory of our baby. I compared them to the newborn photos of Abigail and enjoyed looking at their similarities and differences.

Tim had gone out and my parents left at about half past nine, so I was all alone. It was scary, but I knew I needed to make this step. I watched some television and went for a bath. I lay there soaking in bubbles, and as I unwound, my mind wandered and my head filled with questions that needed answers. But they were not new questions, they were questions that God had already answered.

'Could this really be God's will for us? Was it my fault?' In my tiredness they seemed unanswered again. As I told God what I felt, the Bible verses that had been highlighted in my mind came effortlessly back into my head. I was so grateful for the peace these brought. This happened a lot. Doubts would creep in particularly when I was tired or hungry. I needed continual reassurance: I needed a lot more than just to hear answers once. I needed constant reminding and to hear them afresh, to know that they were true. Sometimes I would leisurely read through the Bible before bed or look up verses I knew well. Those that stood out stayed with me and helped me when I was tempted to think that what had happened was all wrong.

He does what he pleases with the powers of heaven and the peoples of earth. No-one can hold back his hand or say to him: 'What have you done?'[16]

. . . everything he does is right and all his ways are just.[17]

'For my thoughts are not your thoughts, neither are my ways your ways,' declares the Lord. 'As the heavens are higher than the earth, so are my ways higher than your ways and my thoughts than your thoughts.'[18]

This man [Jesus] was handed over to you by God's set purpose and foreknowledge.[19]

Emily's death too, was by God's set purpose and
foreknowledge. God had his reasons, just reasons, and I
wasn't responsible.

5

EMILY'S PLACE

❦

The next day was Wednesday and Mum and Dad would be going home that afternoon. Abigail was getting used to a life of outings and treats and it would be good to return to a more normal routine. It was a hard but necessary step for us all. So it was effectively Tim's and my last morning alone together. We needed to register Emily's death and get started on the funeral arrangements. There was so much to do. We felt the stress of it weighing on us; I had no idea how involved it would be.

Until now, I had never really tasted death. Not properly anyway. I do remember our next door neighbour though. She died when I was five. We were all very fond of her; David, my brother, and I would crawl through the hole in the fence that separated our houses and she would invite us in to play cards and eat sweets. When she died I had cried a little, but that was all. My mum and brother went to her funeral; whether I was considered too young or I just didn't want to go, I don't really know.

Then, over time, my grandparents had each died. I had never known them very well as they lived far away, so again I had only cried a short while, perhaps more for my parent's loss than for mine. I had not wanted to go to the funerals.

Now I was faced with my first funeral. And it was my own daughter's. We had to do more than go; we had to arrange it.

Although it seemed good to have something to do, it was a hard task. Tim could not bear the thought of ringing around undertakers and I was still at the point of being unable to even answer the phone; often too weary for a conversation. We had no idea of what needed to be done. All we had was a preliminary death certificate and an internment request form, whatever that meant.

We had decided we wanted Emily buried. I couldn't bear the thought of her being cremated to ashes. That meant we had to choose and buy a plot of ground in which to bury her. We had to choose a coffin; choose the clothes we wanted her buried in and consider the flowers we liked. We wanted the funeral service in our own church, with our own minister, and this had to be discussed. We needed to fix a time and date for the funeral and we didn't even know when Emily's body would be returned from the postmortem.

Tim's parents rang a couple of funeral parlours that had been recommended by friends to find out about cost and procedure. We were pleased to find that all children's funerals were free; this could also include an unmarked grave in the babies' burial area if this was what was wanted. Some undertakers also provided a car free of charge.

'What did we need cars for?' I wondered. 'Oh yes, a hearse and cars to transport people to and from the funeral and graveside.' There was all so much to think about; clothes, flowers, service, registry, cars, reception. It's no wonder, at times, our tongues slipped and we talked of Emily's wedding!

The first thing we needed to do was register Emily's death. We had made an appointment for this, one that would avoid the time when people were taking their babies and registering births.

We sat and waited in the registry office for quite some time. Although I felt fine when I arrived, the wait was making me nervous and apprehensive. I thought of the time I had come in to register Abigail's birth and how different things were now. I remember having looked at the sad face of an elderly man opposite me and I had thought, 'How awful it must be to come here and register the death of a loved one.' I had never dreamed that so soon, I would be doing the same. The £3.50 was paying for quite a different certificate this time.

The registrar called us in to a big office with two desks. We sat across from her, at the large desk in the middle of the room. We produced the doctor's death certificate and gave her all our details. It took a while and I was pleased when it was over. Emily was entered into a register of stillbirths and my eye caught a glimpse of the previous entry, dated two days ago. I read the name and felt sure that this must be the little baby that had been in the Moses basket beside where we had left Emily. Reading that name, I felt I knew a little about her friend and oddly a little more about Emily. That was nice.

On the way home we passed a funeral parlour and decided to wander in. The display of headstones made me feel a little peculiar. We were taken to a comfortable back room where we made some inquiries and looked at their catalogue of coffins. It all seemed so cold, awkward and ugly; but then, this was death. We needed to decide on a place for the burial too. I had never been to our local cemetery, although I had driven past it many times, always fearing a little any death of my family and friends. I would think what a sad place it must be. What unknown grief was behind those walls. Although I had always believed in heaven and that God watched over my life, the thought of any death was always a thought of dread. Now this unknown was known to me. The fear it had held was dispelled as I marvelled at God's ability to get me through. Without this fear, I felt a new freedom. I would not welcome any more death, but its grip had gone.

We drove up to the gate, entered the small reception and inquired of a heavily pregnant lady: 'Can you tell us where the baby graves are?'

I wondered what she was thinking.

'Have a seat and I'll arrange for someone to show you,' she said. I picked up a few leaflets off a rack. The one entitled 'natural burial area' caught my eye. I quickly scanned it and read that it was burial in an area of the cemetery being created into a nature reserve, where the graves were all unmarked and any memorials were flowers, plants and trees. Tim and I had already discussed whether we wanted a headstone or not. We thought that if we had a headstone and we ever left this town, it would feel like we were leaving something behind, so we had decided against it.

The thought of a baby grave appealed to us. The tiny coffins were all buried together; not between huge adult caskets. I showed Tim this leaflet and hurriedly explained what it was. The lady returned and asked us to go round the back of the crematorium, where someone would be waiting for us.

We could hear the strains of 'The Lord's my Shepherd' coming from the crematorium. Then people started filing out. We tried not to get in the way. We stood looking over the lawns bordered with plaques and flowers, some bright and fresh; others old, dead and wilting. Across the path a man, with whom I presume were two grown up sons, stood waiting also. I wondered who had died in their family; their mother? A grandparent? Sister?

'Oh, it was all so sad.' They appeared very 'together' and I wondered if the death was not a recent one. A man came out of a wooden door behind and walked towards the other people. He noticed us.

'Oh, are you the couple . . .' We nodded.

'I'll go and fetch my colleague.' He disappeared for a second and another man came out. He was a young chap; tall and slim.

'You want to see the baby graves, is that right?'

'Yes.'

'Follow me,' and that is what we did. He marched off at a hare's pace and we trailed behind, trying to keep up. He chatted cheerfully over his shoulder as we went, talking about the cemetery and providing a rather interesting tour.

We came to the top of the hill, it was a new area of cemetery and seemed absolutely packed. The graves were so close together; there didn't seem to be room for a coffin to fit between each headstone. Tim liked the view from the top of the hill, but as we looked at the children's graves we knew this was not where we wanted Emily buried. Plastic bees and whirring windmills covered the area. Many graves were piled high with toys, wet and muddied by the rain; a baby's bottle even lay on one. It spoke of hopelessness and despair; a helpless grasping on to a life that had long since expired. I read some of the headstones; it was so sad, children much older than Emily, who had been known so much longer than we had known Emily, children who had left a great chasm in the lives of their families. I certainly understood the need to keep their memory alive; to do all you can to bury them in a pleasant place, with nice things around them. Yet I wanted to focus on Emily alive in heaven. Not dead in the ground. It was hard to keep focused. It was easy to get drawn into thinking, 'Emily might like that.' But I knew she wasn't there to appreciate it. Now I knew why God had warned me not to get carried away. It was all too easy to turn Emily into something she wasn't. To lose sight of eternity and dwell on death.

We moved on to look at the unmarked graves. As we marched down the hill, I was out of breath; I hadn't done this much exercise for nine months. Tim asked if I was all right. I just nodded, too short of breath to answer. Thinking this must be good for me, I pressed on. I didn't want to embarrass the guy by telling him, 'Slow down, I've just had a baby.' We walked through the older part of the cemetery. The graves here were well spaced out. Headstones were weathered and eroding, tall yew trees and bushes created a natural, warm atmosphere. I felt relaxed. We approached the baby plot and looked on in disappointment. Several graves were now becoming like those at the top of the hill, despite the regulations of 'no headstones', 'unmarked graves only' that were in place. So we asked to be shown the natural burial area. We were led further on and entered a gate to a meadow; tall grass grew, there was a path mowed around the edge where a funeral party had recently walked. Trees and bushes sur-rounded the meadow. It was quiet and still; unspoilt countryside and not a gravestone in sight. The few plaques in the mown path and flowers placed on the grassy banks were the only evidence it was a burial ground. The peace of the place, the natural cycle of life and death that it represented, struck me. I knew this was where I wanted Emily's body to rest.

6

DAY BY DAY

Thursday. My parents weren't here and Tim was popping into work to sort out a few things in the afternoon. While Abigail watched the TV, Tim and I were able to sit down together again. In our Bible reading we read this: 'Suddenly the fingers of a human hand appeared and wrote on the plaster of the wall, near the lampstand in the royal palace. The king watched the hand as it wrote. His face turned pale and he was so frightened that his knees knocked together and his legs gave way.'[20] The writing brought a prophetic message to the king. This reminded me how big and awesome God was. He could do anything. He was sovereign and he was in control. I needed to hear that over and over again. We opened another pile of cards. We were overwhelmed with the love, support and prayers of all our friends and our church congregation. They were there in the midst of our grief, they shared our pain, easing our loneliness. Many cards were filled with Bible verses to encourage us.

'And the God of all grace, who called you to his eternal glory in Christ, after you have suffered a little while, will himself restore you and make you strong, firm and steadfast.'[21] It was so good to read this; no matter how unending our suffering felt now, it would not last, nor would we be destroyed by it.

Amongst the sympathy cards that morning was a birth announcement card from one of my friends. Although lots of my friends were having babies, this one particularly caught me, 'We proudly announce the safe arrival of . . .' I felt gutted. I couldn't be proud of Emily's arrival; instead I felt ashamed at my failure. Yet didn't I know that what had happened was out of my control? Yes, of course I did; I felt God was always telling me that. Hadn't I just been reminded of that half an hour ago?

Still, I remained on the verge of tears all day. I counted up the days, four days since I'd given birth, my 'baby blues' day: I had all the typical feelings of weepiness and depression which are common around the third or fourth day after childbirth – I was terribly, terribly miserable. With Abigail asleep after lunch and Tim at work, I was alone. Added to my misery was guilt. I felt guilty for my self pity. Surely I was only being sad for myself; after all, Emily was quite happy. I tried to get on with various jobs that needed doing. I was sorting through some leaflets for the church when I came across this: 'Be merciful to me, O Lord, for I am in distress; my eyes grow weak with sorrow, my body and soul with grief. . . . But I trust in you O Lord; I say, "You are my God." My times are in your hands.'[22]

As I read, the floodgates of my grief opened. This could have been my distress the psalmist was writing about. It was OK to be sorrowful, it was OK to grieve. I also thought of Jesus, how he wept at the death of his friend Lazarus when he saw the grief of his friends. Also, I thought of the familiar passage in Ecclesiastes; one which I had heard put to music at various times over the years. The tunes went through my head and I looked the words

up in the Bible. 'There is a time for everything, and a season for every activity under heaven: a time to be born and
a time to die, . . . a time to weep and a time to laugh, a
time to mourn and a time to dance, . . . He has made
everything beautiful in its time.'[23] Now was my time to
weep and mourn. When the sobbing eased I looked at
other verses in the leaflet 'Living with Loss',[24] 'Yet not one
of them [sparrows] will fall to the ground apart from the
will of your Father. And even the very hairs of your head
are all numbered. So don't be afraid; you are worth more
than many sparrows.'[25]

Once again I knew Emily's death could not have happened if it was out of God's will. I felt comforted that it
was all in hand – in his hands. The hands of my Father
who loves me.

That night as I bathed Abigail and washed her feet I
was struck by how similar her feet were to Emily's. They
were exactly the same shape, only a little bigger.

'Not really surprising,' Tim said. 'They were sisters.'

'Yes, they were,' I thought, 'real sisters, for a short time
maybe, but an unchangeable fact nonetheless.' I dried
Abigail and remembered Emily's body, her skin that was
so lifeless.

'I will never be able to do this for Emily,' I thought,
'never bathe her or dry her again. Never care for her
needs, never mother her.' It was times like this that I was
unexpectedly thrown back into the reality of my grief, but
that was OK now. Abigail obviously had these times too.
Tim helped get her into bed and read her story.

'Where's Emily?' she asked him.

'She's in heaven,' Tim replied.

Abigail raised her hands high above her head and
answered, 'Up in the air, up in the sky, past the ceil-
ing.'

e had chosen a funeral director and met the undertaker at our home on Friday morning. A young man, no older than us, dressed in a dark suit, entered our house and offered his condolences. His kindly face expressed genuine sympathy and he was sensitive in all his dealings. We led him into our living room; he sat down and, noticing Abigail's toys, chatted about his similarly-aged child. Moving on to the funeral arrangements, he was able to take a lot of our stress away. He would be the one to make many of the phone calls and arrangements for us.

'What makes somebody want to be an undertaker? To deal with death all day long? How could someone want such a morbid profession?' These were questions I had asked myself from time to time, as I walked past the funeral parlours. Now I knew. It was a caring profession, an essential service in the hour of need.

We decided on the small white rectangular casket designed for the stillborn. The inside was satin lined with a pillow; it was bedlike, only there was no getting out. The thought of that lid, firmly in place, made me feel claustrophobic. I tried not to dwell on it. We didn't want to see Emily in the coffin. We wanted to remember her as she had been when she was born. I preferred to imagine what the inside of that coffin was like. I did not want to be confronted with the stark reality of her body prettily dressed under six feet of earth. After all, Emily wasn't really trapped in that suffocating place, she was in heaven with bright light and shining glory.

We hired just one car for Tim, myself and the coffin. Being a small casket, only one pallbearer was necessary, and he was the driver. The car was a white limousine that would pick us up and take us to the church. I had thought, for some reason, that coffins were already at the church; it was nice to think that 'we' would all arrive together. We were shown a catalogue of flower arrangements and I was drawn to the highly priced teddy made of white flowers, I was tempted to get this for Emily, but reminded myself that she wouldn't see it. I tried to focus on the simple funeral that Tim and I had agreed upon. We asked our family and friends who wanted to give flowers to send simple sprays. Our flowers, we wanted to do ourselves.

We needed to think about a small reception as some people were travelling a long distance. What a thing for grieving people to do: throw a party! We didn't feel up to this at all. Many people had said to us, 'Let us know if there is anything we can do to help.' Jane, Tim's sister, older than Tim by two years, offered to have people back to her house. She and her husband John and their two girls had recently moved to a new house. It was large and ideal for the reception. We would still need some help providing the food so we asked our house group to provide a finger buffet. Our house group is a small group of people from our church who meet locally, midweek, in someone's house for Bible studies, prayer and social activities. Everyone was only too pleased to help and we were very grateful. It was one less thing to worry about.

Now I needed some new clothes. All my usual clothes were too small and the last thing I wanted to do was wear my maternity ones. Not being pregnant, not holding a baby yet wearing maternity clothes can be a confusing embarrassment! I did not want to look like I was in early pregnancy. I wanted a new dress for the funeral and in my mind's eye I could see just what I wanted.

A few days later we set out to try and find it. The shops were busy and hot. In one shop, Tim had gone downstairs with Abigail to look in the men's section. I waited by the door; in walked a couple with a newborn baby in its harness. I stood there, glancing over every now and again with tears pricking my eyes. The baby began to cry and the mother made frantic efforts to keep it quiet. When I saw this I felt less sad, I remembered those hard days when Abigail had cried endlessly. Finally, we would think she had stopped, then she would start all over again, or else she would giggle and gurgle when all of us should have been asleep. We continued wandering round the shops.

'This shop has a closing down sale,' I noticed, 'maybe there will be something in here.' The shop was hot. Abigail was bored and I felt sick and frustrated. I felt like shouting, 'I've got to buy a dress for my daughter's funeral.' I searched through the racks and finally found several possibilities. Their summer stock had been put out at much reduced prices. Then I found it; just what I had in mind. Nevertheless, I carried all seven dresses to the fitting rooms! Abigail came with me and took all her clothes off! She dressed up in the oversized garments and had a great time, only disappointed that they weren't being bought for her.

'They're too big,' I kept explaining. Tim waited patiently outside and reviewed each of my dresses in turn. He said they all looked good. I chose the special one I had found and Tim also persuaded me to buy another. I didn't really feel like it but nevertheless I didn't need a great deal of persuasion! The lady at the checkout admired the dress; never contemplating the occasion for which it was bought.

My dress hugged my still too large figure, but somehow managed to hide my bulging stomach. It was black; a symbol of my mourning. It was splashed with vibrant red roses; the rosebuds reminded me of Emily's full-coloured lips, and the flowers, of her fleeting beauty. The bright colour coming out of the blackness made me think of hope, of heaven and the joy I felt, knowing she was there. The dress stopped just above the knee and was sleeveless. I had a black jacket I could wear with it. I knew I would still be cold but that seemed unimportant. Tim bought a dark grey tie, with lighter, brighter squares patterned across it. Pleased with our purchases we went home.

A couple of days later Martin came to see us again and we planned the funeral service. Tim and I especially wanted to share with everyone how good God was. How he was helping us through. That in the sadness, there was celebration because our dear Emily was in heaven. We wanted to share with our friends that this paradise was waiting for them too and that God is always at our side whenever we call.

⚜

A week had passed since that dreadful day. The funeral was prepared and looming ahead like a big dark cloud. It wouldn't be long before Tim was back at work and life had to return to its more usual pattern. We had spent so much time sharing our feelings with each other, we had our grief in common and we were glued together. It felt like falling in love all over again. One afternoon, as Abigail slept, we returned to our bed. Yet our first love-making ended in tears. Tim held me tight as I cried, 'There's no Emily in between us.' At first my body didn't long for Tim: instead, I longed for my baby – my body ached to feed her.

Over the next few days I tried to do a few chores by myself with Abigail, so it would seem less daunting when Tim was not around.

I walked around the supermarket and saw people who had 'complete' families. I thought, 'Why? Why can they have their second child, when I can't? It's not fair.' God replied to my envy, quite gently, ['When Peter saw him, he asked, "Lord what about him?" Jesus answered,] ". . .*what is that to you*? You must follow me."'[26]

I was then sorry for my jealousy and I knew I was forgiven: 'If we confess our sins, he is faithful and just and will forgive us our sins and purify us from all unrighteousness.'[27] I was able to move on, another issue dealt with. No guilt, no bitterness, no resentment.

I knew the theory of grief, I had studied its stages at school: denial, acceptance, anger, guilt. I knew it was accepted to be angry, yet I did not want to become embittered or allow any feelings to spoil my relationship with God. So I often prayed that God would protect my grief, that he would not allow Satan to interfere with it by causing me to doubt God's love, justice and sovereignty.

When Abigail slept in the afternoons I had some time to rest quietly and pray. Then I would sometimes try some antenatal exercises. I had asked the midwife for these; without a baby to feed, I wondered if my figure would ever return to normal. I am very bad at any sort of exercising and on this very rare occasion I lay on the floor with my knees bent up pulling my tummy muscles in and out, in and out. As I repeated these movements, my thoughts turned towards Abigail who lay snoring in the room next door. I grieved for her.

'Her sister has gone. Surely she is missing out?' I said to God. It had seemed the perfect time for her to have a sibling. She needed a companion, someone to share her childhood with, and of course, she needed to learn to share! But God loved Abigail too. His promises applied to her as well. The plans he has for her life are to prosper her and not to harm her, too, so she would not be harmed by what had happened. I felt relieved by this. Relieved knowing that God knew Abigail's needs and when they had to be met. He would make sure she didn't go without either.

'And my God will meet all your needs according to his glorious riches in Christ Jesus.'[28] In fact, God knows what these needs are much more than we do, because unlike us, he can see the whole picture, our lives spread out in front of him. 'His thoughts are higher than mine.'

I thought back to Abigail's statement earlier that day, 'Emily won't be needing her cot now, will she Mummy?' She was obviously working through what had happened. Realising that Abigail was grieving in her own way and having to cope with her own disappointment helped me to love her when it was hard. She had become very silly and was having lots of tantrums. She was always right in my face demanding something, just when I needed peace and quiet. It felt like I had lost my little Abigail too.

People used to say to me, 'At least you've still got Abigail, that must help.' But it didn't always. Abigail could never be Emily. It was Emily that I was missing and Abigail could not fill that gap. Of course deep down I loved Abigail but sometimes I would get very cross with her and shout and scream at her. She never deserved that. Calm discipline, yes, but not uncontrolled anger. The joy and pride that she had always brought me disappeared. I felt guilty. Why was I feeling like this? It certainly wasn't something that I wanted to admit to. It was hard to talk about, hard to ask about. Hard to let go of. I prayed that God would help me, forgive my lack of love and restore that joy and love that I'd had for Abigail. I persevered at loving whether I felt like it or not. The Bible commands us to love and tells us how to do it in 1 Corinthians 13:4–8. It's helpful to know that sometimes we need instruction to love, that love is an act of will rather than emotion, particularly at the times when we are very emotionally vulnerable. I tried to be calm and patient. Putting her need for controlled discipline, for activities to be set up for her before my need to sit down and be alone. This was not easy. I was tempted to think I would never have any of the time I needed. Sometime later I read the story of Jesus feeding the five thousand. The situation in which this miracle happened made me sit up and take note. Jesus had needed space, needed time on his own; he had just heard that John the Baptist had been beheaded. So he went privately by boat to a solitary place, but when he got there he found that a crowd of people had followed him on foot. Yet he didn't say, 'Oh no, what about my time alone, my space?' Instead he had compassion on the people and healed them. Perhaps my favourite bit of this story is that God still knew that he needed this solitude, even though he had to wait a little bit longer than expected. For, after Jesus dismissed the crowd, he went up on a mountainside to pray and there he was alone at last. His need for solitude was met, even though he put others first. This was a wonderful realisation, knowing that as I put Abigail first, God would meet my own needs for the times of quiet. They might be postponed a little, but they would still be found. I planned some quality time with Abigail, when it was just her and me with no distractions. We went to the park and fed the ducks, we sat on the bench overlooking the lake and I listened to her chatter. We ran around and played on the swings. I enjoyed her company again. God had restored our relationship.

Later that evening I sat on the sofa and watched Abigail play.

'Can I take my toys to heaven?' she asked

'Oh, well you won't need them,' I replied. 'Heaven's full of fun things to do.'

'Can I go there now?'

'No, not yet.'

'Tomorrow?'

'No, not for a very long time, we've got lots to do here first.'

Abigail wanted what Emily already had. That was comforting. Abigail continued to play her imaginative games, her endless chatter, all so full of character.

'I will never even know Emily like this,' I thought, 'I'll not know what she's like, not know who she is.' I sighed. 'I will never see her grow up.' I wondered how old she would be in heaven. I was sad for me, then suddenly sad for Emily.

'Will she be able to appreciate it as a baby?' I thought with panic. Initially I settled for the answer, 'Well, heaven is perfect, she'll be fine,' but I found myself searching for much deeper answers, for further proof and clarity of my vague statement.

7

THE FUNERAL

❧

Emily, our millennium child, was buried on Friday 1st December 2000, twelve days after her birth; twelve, maybe thirteen, days after her death. She wore a bright pink sleepsuit. Buried with her was her fluffy white rabbit, the bottoms of its paws were made from mauve, embroidered material. I did not want to think of Emily's body being all alone in the grave. The rabbit was my favourite cuddly toy, precious to me. By burying that too, I felt I was showing in a small way how much I loved Emily.

On Thursday evening, we had driven to the supermarket, and chosen a bunch of pale pink and cream flowers. They had just seemed right for Emily; they were soft and beautiful, warm and rich, yet cut from their root. They would blossom only to live a short while and then wilt and fade into the ground. I got them home and arranged them in a spray to fit on top of the coffin. I found some pink ribbon and tied them together. I liked arranging the flowers myself; I did it just the way I wanted.

When we went to bed that night my nerves were like pre-wedding jitters; only there was none of the joyful anticipation, no excitement. We each took a sleeping pill, encouraging our minds to rest.

The morning brought with it dreary skies and drizzle.

'Very fitting,' I thought, as I took Abigail off to her nursery for the day. She didn't usually go on a Friday, but we had decided after prayerful consideration that it was better she didn't attend the funeral. I had initially been very keen that she was involved in all aspects of Emily's death. I felt she would miss out otherwise. But my father had given me this wise analogy: 'Just as a child is not physically strong, unable to carry a heavy chair, in the same way a young child is not emotionally strong. A lifeless body, her sister in a box, being put in the ground and everyone crying; it is too big a burden for her to bear.'

Abigail had already accepted that Emily was in heaven. I think she believed that she had ascended there, just like Jesus. Only Emily, she thought, had come out of my tummy and floated up into the air. Abigail didn't need to be confused with the details that it was Emily's spirit that had gone to heaven and her body that needed to be buried. The full truth would be revealed in time as she grew up.

After I'd settled Abigail into nursery, Tim and I realised what enormous stress we were under, as tensions built up. I went to pick up Tim from his sister's. He had gone to park his car there, so that we would have transport back from the funeral reception. The road was being resurfaced; it was full of potholes and workmen had left only a narrow passage to get past, so I waited in the car a little way away from their house. I hadn't wanted to be spotted anyway; I didn't feel like making conversation. Tim drove up and parked on their drive, then he walked back to my car. He was annoyed and upset. Raising his voice he said, 'Why didn't you come and pick me up?'

'I didn't know I was supposed to,' I retorted.

'But it's pouring with rain.'

'I didn't think,' I had noticed it rain harder, but I hadn't considered that Tim might be getting wet.

'You never do . . .'

The argument continued and got more and more heated, we were both shouting and getting upset. It carried on all the way home, 'I'm not going to the funeral, you can go by yourself,' I said. We were just about to turn into our road. 'What did you tell them?' I asked.

'That I didn't know why you were parked so far away.'

'You liar. You did know, I told you.'

With those words of mine Tim had left the car and slammed the door before I was able to stop him. Our neighbour's car was coming towards us – they had seen it all. I turned the corner and pulled over. I wasn't going home. That would show him. I sat there stony faced, the hour of the funeral fast approaching.

'How could I drive past the neighbours now?' The whole day had been spoilt, not that it was to be a nice day, but still it was even worse now.

I sat there and thought how God had carried me through my grieving and now look what I was doing. I was shutting him out, not listening to his way; I was arguing, being selfish, proud and stubborn.

This was just what Satan would have wanted, to get me to ruin everything and I needed to stop.

It was obvious that Tim and I were both very anxious about the funeral, without actually realising it. We were arguing about something so silly. I turned the ignition, went into first gear, released the handbrake, second gear, third gear and drove the short distance home. Tim was in the kitchen making himself a cup of coffee. It was hard to go in; I hate backing down, I'm too proud. It was also hard seeing him doing something normal, apparently unperturbed, while I was fuming.

'I'm sorry,' I said rather ungraciously.

'I am too. You don't think I'm a liar then?'

'Of course not!' I softened – Tim had been hurt by my words. 'I was just reacting. I am coming to the funeral.'

'So you lied then?'

'Yes. Do you want to make up?'

'I thought we just had.'

'No, I mean really make up?' I smiled shyly.

⌘

We were ready and sitting waiting for the limousine to arrive. I couldn't sit still. I was becoming more and more nervous. My biggest concern was how I would react when I saw the coffin.

Then I saw it. The white car slowly edged past our window. I looked out and caught a glimpse of the coffin, small and white, like a large shoe box, sitting in the middle of the back seat.

'OK, I've seen it now,' I said to myself. 'I know what to expect.'

There was a quiet knock at the door and I was pleased to see the undertaker we knew. Everything then seemed to go into slow motion. We handed him our flowers and he went to put them on top of the coffin. I picked up my handbag and stepped outside. We closed the front door and got into the limousine as the doors were held open. We sat on the soft, cream leather with the coffin between us. On the seats in front were all the flowers from our friends and family, but we could not see them properly; the back of the seat in front obscured them from our view. It was now that I felt a twinge of regret at not seeing what Emily looked like inside the coffin, but the lid was firmly sealed. At the same time, I knew that I didn't really want to see. I felt the smooth, solid wood with my fingers and read the pale pink plaque:

Baby Emily Ruth Lycett, 19th November 2000.

The car pulled slowly out of the drive and drove on to the church. I avoided the looks of passers-by. We arrived at the church and the undertaker got out. He took the coffin stands into the chapel and I took the opportunity to look at all the beautiful flowers; there were clusters of cream and pink roses, white lilies and pink forget-me-nots. I read the greetings and felt tears burning my eyes. My door opened. It was time to go.

We stood waiting by the car as the undertaker picked up Emily's coffin. Martin, our minister, came out of the chapel to meet us. I looked at him, I looked at the coffin, I looked at everyone's sorrowful faces and began to cry. I buried my sobs in Tim's chest and the funeral which was due to start at twelve noon had to wait a little longer.

We followed the coffin into the church; I kept my head down. I wanted to know who was there, but I could not make eye contact. We sat down at the front and the opening hymn began.

> *The Lord's my shepherd, I'll not want;*
> *He makes me down to lie*
> *In pastures green;*
> *He leadeth me*
> *The quiet waters by.*

My soul He doth restore again;
And me to walk doth make
Within the paths of righteousness,
E'en for His own name's sake.
Yea, though I walk in death's dark vale,
Yet will I fear no ill;
For Thou art with me; and Thy rod
And staff me comfort still.

My table Thou hast furnished
In the presence of my foes;
My head Thou dost with oil anoint,
And my cup overflows.

Goodness and mercy all my life
Shall surely follow me;
And in God's house for evermore
My dwelling place shall be.[29]

I let the tears stream unchecked down my face; those words, I sang quietly, as they ministered joy into my soul. I was joyful because God was taking me unscathed through death's dark place, he was restoring me and giving me all the comfort, peace and hope that I needed. How I looked forward to being with him for ever. Martin read Psalm 84 and explained to everyone how we had felt God speak to us through it when we were in hospital. He was choking on the words, overcome with emotion. I was pleased I had decided not to read it myself. I could just sit and listen. As I listened, I was thrown back into that hospital room, the time when Tim rushed to my side as I sobbed over my Bible. I was aware again of the closeness of God beside me, his love overwhelming me and I knew the joyful reassurance that Emily was with him and one day I would be there too. We sang the next song. It was full of yet more powerful words.

> Faithful one so unchanging, Ageless one you're my rock of peace.
> Lord of all I depend on you, I call out to you again and again.
> I call out to you again and again.
> You are my rock in times of trouble.
> You lift me up when I fall down.
> All through the storm your love is the anchor,
> My hope is in you alone.[30]

How true this song was, what an expression of my experience of God.

The minister began: 'I've been to many a funeral where a person has reached a good old age, their life is celebrated by listing their many achievements . . . but that's not how it is today . . . yet Emily Ruth has done something that has affected us all; her life has spoken to us. She has left us something to remember her by.

'She grew and developed, woke, slept and was nourished, she discovered what it was to be totally dependent on someone else; her mother. Her life was lived in an attitude of complete trust. She experienced profound love as she was nurtured in the womb.

'As Christians we believe that everyone is made in the image of God . . . Emily Ruth lived a short life of love and trust . . . these are surely among the greatest human qualities. Love and trust are things God wants us to know about himself. He loves us with an everlasting love; he is utterly trustworthy.

'The Bible shows us that unborn life is precious to God. Psalm 139:13 says to God "you knit me together in my mother's womb." The miracle of life is God's handiwork. Isaiah 49:1 says "Before I was born the Lord called me; from my birth he has made mention of my name." At twenty weeks Tim and Debs named their daughter and Isaiah says God also called her by name.

'Some might say, "But Emily never spoke to us". Well not in an audible voice, but I believe her life asks us a question: Is this life all there is? . . . If it is then there's a great injustice, but Jesus Christ gives us the confidence to believe in a greater, more wonderful, more joyful, eternal life. ". . . if I go and prepare a place for you, I will come back and take you to be with me". He himself endured death and then rose to life again, to prove that death does not have the last word. The Bible promises us that heaven is a place where we dwell in God's presence for ever. Where "He will wipe [away] every tear from their eyes. There will be no more death or mourning or crying or pain". . . . Emily has not been snatched unfairly, but has been given so soon what the rest of us wait a lifetime for. Of course we have a natural longing for her to be here with us, but we know that she is in an infinitely better place . . . We are wise to ask if we too are ready to meet our Maker when our time comes.

'We may feel that we don't have much to remember her by . . . I want to suggest we could all remember her by this one thing. Emily Ruth left nothing undone that she should have done. In the innocence of a small baby, not yet born, she moved from this life to the next, having done all that she needed to do. She did not leave this life with regrets or unfinished business . . . Perhaps we could honour her memory by remembering the fragility of our own lives and the need to seize each day and make the most of it, while we still have the chance. For us we may need to sort out relationships, forgive someone, keep a promise or sort out our relationship with God, to be prepared to meet him. Psalm 90:12 says "Teach us to number our days aright, that we may gain a heart of wisdom." We are prone to overestimate our days, thinking there will always be time to sort things out. Let's learn from Emily and leave nothing undone.'[31]

The service concluded with a prayer of thanks for Emily's life; a plea for help in our grief and a new understanding of God's eternal love and life for us all. We sang the final song, 'There is a Redeemer' and walked out to its echo.

> When I stand in glory,
> I will see His face.
> And there I'll serve my King for ever,
> in that Holy Place.[32]

8

THE PROMISE

utside, I was once again overcome with emotion as I hugged my mother. We got into the cars. I waved to some of my friends as we drove off. I wanted to talk to everybody, to say hello, but many friends felt unable to come to the graveside, so I had to wait until I saw them again. I was saddened as I saw all their grief and wished I could comfort them too, as I had been comforted. It was pouring with rain and very, very cold. I thought, for the second time, 'How fitting,' and also, 'we're going to freeze!'

We drove to the cemetery and right up to the graveside, my parents' car close behind and Tim's parents behind them, then more family after that. It was a long queue of cars in a very narrow muddy lane.

We were given an umbrella and walked behind the coffin. As we entered the meadow I heard the birds singing; they seemed louder than I had ever noticed birds to sing before. We walked towards the deep hole. The bare earth had been covered by a green blanket of Astroturf and wooden planks made the muddy ground solid beneath our feet. I looked down the hole. I needed to see and take everything in; there would be no opportunity later. I didn't want to have any wondering regrets of what it was like down there. At the bottom of the neat hole there was a sea of colour; many flowers had been scattered on top of the soil, hiding the cold ugliness of the grave. The grave was dug under a large yew tree and sitting on its trunk was a bird house. The spot was nicer than we had imagined.

We stood around shivering with cold. I had one arm around my mother and with the other I was clinging to Tim. The rain was pouring down. Ever so slowly, the little coffin was lowered into the ground. Our minister was talking and then praying. I was so transfixed by what was going on that I could only half listen: at the very moment the coffin touched the bottom of the grave; the rain suddenly stopped. The sun shone in all its brilliance. Bright light and heat bathed our faces. All I could do, was hold my face up to its intense warmth and radiance. It was a long time before I could turn away. That, to me, was a symbol of God's glory. An outward sign that he was really there, that he cared and that what had happened was all right because he was indeed in control and was bigger and above all things. He had shown me his glory from the sky and I knew that Emily was right there, at home with him, not enjoying mere sunshine, but in the *fullness* of his glory. I was filled with hope and happiness. I turned around. I wanted to see who else had arrived.

As I turned, there in front of me was a startling rainbow. The whole of it was visible – its beginning rose to an enormous arch that spanned the sky, its end touched the horizon. My mother was clearly taken aback; unable to contain her excitement she said, 'God's promised. No more dead babies; it's not going to happen again.'

'Why is she saying that?' I thought. 'Why is she telling me that, now? Of course I would love it to be true, and yes, the shining sun and the rainbow are undeniably timely. But how does she know that this is what it means?'

Excitedly, she spoke into my ear, 'Last week, as we walked along the beach at Sandbanks, we saw a rainbow. I felt that God said to me, that it was a sign of his promise. He would not let this happen again. But I said to God, "Oh, you are going to have to show me that again, I need to see it one more time before I can really believe and accept it." And I'd completely forgotten about it until now. Yet there it is; another rainbow and God's promise that it won't happen again.'

Now I believed; I cried all over again, so joyful, so hopeful.

We stood around for a little while; looking at the flowers and reading the messages, hugging each other and crying together. I did not want to leave that spot. I didn't want to leave the rainbow behind, but it was time to go. As we walked down the path my mum told Tim about the rainbow too. Back in the car I asked him, 'What did you think about what my Mum said?'

'God seems to have told me the same thing. Last night when I was reading Noah's ark to Abigail, we read about the rainbow and I, too, felt that God was promising us that this wouldn't happen again.'

'Wow.' God seemed to have told Tim too – that confirmed it even more.

I sat back in my seat; the floor was muddy now. There was no little coffin between us and it felt empty. The cars squeezed round the cemetery lanes and out on to the main road. We drove at normal speed now to Jane and John's. When we arrived we took off our muddy shoes and we went in. The dining room table was laden with buffet food; friends and family stood and sat, chatting as they ate. The atmosphere was cheerful. I felt such relief that the funeral was over; all that stress could now be left behind.

'Oh, brie, I can eat that now,' I said. I had carefully avoided it for nine long months.

'You can eat absolutely anything you like now,' Jane agreed warmly. It was little consolation, I know, but I'd found when the big things were taken away the little things meant more.

When we went home, my parents came too and we exchanged our Christmas presents. I fumbled in the bottom of our wardrobe where I had hidden them. I tried to remember which presents were whose. I hadn't labelled them, thinking I would easily remember. After shaking them I realised that several were of course Emily's. I had done all the Christmas shopping in early November, so that I didn't have to do it when Emily was just born, when I would be exhausted, short of sleep and dealing with all the demands of a newborn baby and toddler. I put Emily's presents back, but all I thought was 'I must get this right, it would be no good Mum or Dad opening Emily's teething keys.'

Mum and Dad left shortly after having a cup of tea – they wanted to avoid the traffic – and I went to pick up Abigail from nursery. The hard day was over. Now, whenever I felt sad, there was a new feeling as well: relief. 'It's all over. I can move on,' I thought, but it wasn't as easy as that; even then, there was a little niggle. A nagging feeling that I couldn't quite put my finger on.

❧

The next day was Saturday. Abigail went for her afternoon nap and I decided to return to the cemetery. As I drove across town I felt nervous and nauseated, but I didn't really know why. I parked in the car park and wandered slowly through the trees and graves. As I approached the meadow I could see her grave through the fence. It was piled high with fresh earth; rich, dark soil, and it was topped with a blaze of bright colour where the flowers had been lain. This first glimpse of the grave brought fresh tears to my eyes and a deep heartache. I walked slowly on. There were very few people about and those that were there were feeling their losses too. I could sense a common, unspoken bond of grief between us. I entered the meadow at the gate and picked my way through the mud. I absorbed the peace and tranquillity around me; it was late in the afternoon, the sun was setting and the birds beginning to roost. They sang their evening song as I sat down on the fence and wept.

'My daughter's under there,' I thought, 'her little body that I grew and carried for nine months.' I rearranged the flowers and reread all the little cards. I pocketed some of those special words, 'Always remembering our dear little Emily, safe with Jesus, we will see you again. Love Grandma and Granddad.'

It was getting chilly. I stood and watched the sun setting behind Emily's tree, recalling yesterday's promise of hope. I remembered God's love and reassurance that Emily was OK, that she was at home with him.

I hung around until I felt there was no further point being there. Then I walked around the rest of the meadow, reading the paving stones of other graves. I needed to know the place a little better. I went out of the gate, wiping the mud off my shoes. I had developed a very slow gait and I thoughtfully and leisurely made my way back to the car. I was feeling a lot better; the release of emotion had given me peace. That quiet time at the graveside, alone with my thoughts of Emily had taken away that nagging feeling; the feeling that something was left undone.

I sat in the car for a while before going back home. I was wrestling again with the need to return to Abigail when I just wanted to stay here and love Emily.

I listened to 'Emily's Song' on the radio as I drove. I'd heard this song, 'My Love' by Westlife, played often now; I had made it Emily's song, because it expressed my sadness and caused me to think of heaven, that better place, that beautiful place far away where I would see Emily again.

9

MOVING ON

❧

On Sunday morning, I woke up to find orange blotches on my nightie: my breasts were leaking.

This went on for about a week despite medication to prevent it. Even without any conscious thought about feeding her, my breasts contracted and milk dripped out every time I would talk or think of Emily.

We went to church; it was easier this week than last. Last week I had cried and cried through the prayers, especially those that were for us. The worship had been uplifting though and it was good to face people before we would have to see them all at the funeral. Everyone had been so encouraged to see us there; when they spoke to me I could see the tears in their own eyes. Now that the hardest part of meeting most people for the first time had been done, this morning proceeded uneventfully. Then we invited Fred and Margaret around after church. We didn't want to be alone. We had no food so they stopped off at the supermarket on the way. They brought pizzas, salad and apple strudel. That was the first meal I really enjoyed.

With the funeral behind us, we decided to spend a day out on Tuesday, a day away from the house. Somewhere new, somewhere different. Somewhere with no memories of Emily. A place to bond as a family. A family of just three.

Ignoring the pouring rain, we travelled into the Forest of Dean. We put the seats down and climbed into the back of the estate car. There we sat and read with our backs resting against the side of the car and our legs stretched out in front of us. Abigail took plenty of her books and dolls with her, but most of the time she sat in the front seat. She had her seatbelt fastened securely and she drove us all to the shops and back again. Several times!

We took the opportunity to read the Bible. I was getting annoyed and frustrated. My mind was tired; day after day, I churned through what had happened, trying to make sense of it until I could no longer think straight.

'I must be going mad,' I thought. 'Why is this so hard? Why such a battle within me?' I worried that my faith would not stand such a time of testing. As I read the Bible, sitting in the back of the car, I stopped worrying. This is what God showed me: 'Do not be anxious about anything, but in everything, by prayer and petition, with thanksgiving, present your requests to God. And the peace of God, which transcends all understanding, *will guard your hearts and minds in Christ Jesus.*'[33] My heart, where my faith is; and my mind, my sanity, would be protected.

Also as I read more of the Bible, these two words struck me, '. . . endure hardship . . .'[34]

'That's OK then,' I thought, 'it's not wrong to find things hard, we are asked to endure.'

The rain eased off for a little while and we put on our boots and macs. We walked up a hill which spiralled behind us; at the top was a viewpoint. A large gravelled circle with a short wall around the edge marked the spot. Abigail ran and ran around the inside of the circle. Tim and I stood and waited, getting a little wetter with each lap, but thinking that such good exercise would tire Abigail out for the journey home. We walked down the other side through the pine trees and were going on into the forest. I could have walked for hours: I loved the fresh, crisp air, the smell of damp pine, the peace and privacy of the wood. But Abigail was getting tired and her whinge-ing and crying took us quickly back to the car; here we fin-ished off the remains of our picnic and headed home.

The next day I returned to the Wednesday morning Parents and Toddlers group. Everyone shared condo-lences with me and I felt uplifted; I was able to share with all my friends how God had helped me through and the sadness was lightened a little more. Then someone came over to me.

'It happened to me too, you know,' she said. A virtually identical situation, only four years before, the same mid-wives, the same induction of birth, the same hospital, the same cemetery. It helped so much to share my experience: one that was understood down to the finest detail. I felt relief. The feeling of isolation, the feeling of being an out-cast, that there was something strange about me, some-thing wrong with me, because everyone else ended up with their babies and I hadn't, disappeared. I had not even known I was feeling this until it went; when I knew I was not the only one, not even the only one in this circle of friends. I hadn't known how much I needed to meet this lady, but God had known. I went home. Tim was in the garage working on restoring his Austin A40, and I excit-edly told him about my morning.

At the weekend I wanted to pack Emily's room away. This was part of my moving on. I also felt it would help to consolidate things in Abigail's mind. Abigail and I set about the task.

It seemed a good day in terms of emotional sadness; I wasn't brimming over with tears, but I did feel fraught and stressed. I found it hard deciding what to put back in the loft, what to give away and what to keep where it was. In the end I decided that anything that would gather dust must be put away. Equipment that was nearing the end of its life, unlikely to last for more than one more baby, I packed for the loft. Then I thought, 'No. This really should come back down. How selfish! I have friends who might be in need of this.' I remembered this Bible verse, 'All the believers were together and had everything in common. Selling their possessions and goods, they *gave* to anyone as he had need.'[35]

Had I not read recently that God would meet all our needs? 'We shall not be in want later and they must not be in want now.' This was a small challenge, but hard because I thought I knew what was best for us. I wanted to do what I wanted and not question it. That was a failing.

Eventually I said to my friends they could have whatever they needed and I was left with more than enough!

Over the months before Emily's birth, the baby clothes Abigail had worn were carefully washed and folded into the drawers. The newborn sleepsuits, I placed in the top together with the winter, woolly cardigans and booties. The next drawer was for three to six months old clothing and the bottom drawer was packed with summer dresses from six months. All these clothes were left untouched. They awaited further use when the time came. I did not have the heart to pack them away.

'They will come to no harm where they are,' I thought.

Abigail played for a while with Emily's toys and then we packed them all away. Abigail was very disappointed not only to see the toys go away, but to see that Emily's home was not here.

'They are for Emily,' she said.

'Yes, but she doesn't need them now. She has a room in heaven. Do you remember that Jesus is in heaven getting our rooms ready?' I asked. It was very special for me to remember this. Instead of thinking, 'Oh, her lovely room, it's so sad, she's left her room behind,' I thought: 'Her room was prepared in heaven, and she is enjoying a much better one there.' Because Jesus said: 'In my Father's house are many rooms; if it were not so I would have told you. I am going there to prepare a place for you. And if I go and prepare a place for you, I will come back and take you to be with me that you also may be where I am. You know the way to the place where I am going.'[36]

I went back into Emily's room that night and drew the curtains. Each time I did this I felt a little sad.

The next day we went to church as usual. On the way home I turned to Tim.

'Do you remember our conversation, here, a few months ago? I told you that I had committed Emily to God; just like we did with Abigail.' That service had talked about generosity and encouraged us to consider what we could give to God. I realised we hadn't voiced our desire that Emily would belong to God; I did so then. It was that we were just looking after her for him. It was a bit like when Hannah, in the Bible, asked God for a son and promised to give him to God. She wanted his whole life to be lived in fruitful service to him. When Samuel was old enough, Hannah took her son to the priest and there he served God in the temple; where God called him to be his prophet. This was Hannah's prayer when he dedicated Samuel to God: 'I prayed for this child, and the Lord has granted me what I asked of him. So now I give him to the Lord. For his whole life he shall be given over to the Lord.'[37]

As I remembered that we had given Emily to God, I felt that it was even more OK that she was with him. It was better that she was with him in heaven now and for ever, than she lived a long life in this world, perhaps becoming disillusioned, attracted by Satan's sugar-coated temptations, never bothering to get to know God and ending up spending eternity separated from him. A place without God would be terrible. It would after all be a place without light and without love, because when God is not there the source of these things has gone. A place without love, without any expression of love, is a place where there is no patience, no kindness, no hope, no trust, no truth, only pride and envy, selfishness and greed, anger and revenge, fear, pain and sorrow. For love is summed up like this: 'Love is patient, love is kind. It does not envy, it does not boast, it is not proud. It is not rude, it is not self-seeking, it is not easily angered, it keeps no record of wrongs. Love does not delight in evil but rejoices in the truth. It always protects, always trusts, always hopes, always perseveres. Love never fails.'[38] A place without light and love is where there is no friendship – 'But if we walk in the light, as he [God] is in the light, we have fellowship with one another, and the blood of Jesus, his Son, purifies us from all sin.'[39]

10

PICKING UP THE PIECES

onday morning, Tim was returning to work and I had to pick up my old routine. Normally I would try to take Abigail out each morning shopping, going to toddler groups or meeting friends for Bible study and prayer. In the afternoons Abigail went to bed and I had my rest, which I had needed being pregnant. Now, the thought of going back to all this without Emily, cut into me deeply. I didn't want to pick up where I had left off. I wanted to move on with my new baby. I felt so empty.

'What do I do now?' I had planned and set everything up, created an Emily shaped space in my life and now it was a gaping chasm, with nothing to fill it. I felt depressed and bored: there was no joy in doing any-thing. I have always been the sort of person who puts so much effort into things that, should I fail, I would not have the heart to try again. When I was doing my 'A' levels, someone asked me, 'If you fail will you repeat them?'

'No!' I had replied hotly. 'I won't fail, I can't fail.' If I did then I was incapable of ever passing them; so intense had been my efforts that I couldn't possibly have tried any harder!

At twenty-two I'd failed my driving test and I had been completely devastated. I had never failed anything before and I was convinced that I would never be able to drive. I had tried so hard so surely I just couldn't do it! I was a little comforted by the fact that many people fail their driving test the first time and so, out of the desperate need to be able to drive (Tim was doing an hour's round trip to take me and pick me up from work each day), I tried again; that time I passed.

Now, it felt like I had to repeat a year. I was feeling more and more like I still wanted another baby and I felt so left behind in my plans. It helped when I remembered about God's plans for my life. His plans were bigger than mine and they were to prosper me and not to harm me. That meant this gap didn't matter because God knew all about it; he understood what was going on and he was in control. I found such freedom in accepting to live according to his will, rather than striving to achieve my own goals; which in fact would not be the best for me if I could see the whole picture and which I had no real control over anyway. God had given me hope for even better things – in what ways, I did not know, but it was a hope I held on to.

Without having Emily to look after, I was getting unbroken nights of sleep. I was not so tired and Abigail's growing independence allowed me time to myself; if only I knew how to fill it.

Monday is the day for food shopping. The supermarket is quiet and our fridge is empty after the weekend. I walked around doing my weekly shop with Abigail; everything reminded me that Emily was missing. The stark reality hit me in the face as I remembered the last time we did this. We had spent ages in the baby aisle. Pointing to the dummies, 'Which ones do you think Emily would like?' I had asked Abigail. She had pondered a while and chosen the teddy-decorated pacifiers.

Now, having struggled around the shop, choosing food with one hand and grabbing Abigail with the other as she dashed in front of the trolleys, I pushed my heavily laden trolley towards the till. I was getting nervous. Would those at the checkout remember me? Would they ask?

'Oh, you've had your baby I see. Was it a boy or a girl?'

No one did ask. Instead I was a mother with only one child. Someone who didn't need help with packing her shopping or taking it to the car – but I wasn't and I did!

The next day I met up with a friend whose first baby was born two weeks after mine and whose second baby, also a girl, was born four days after Emily. We had met up several times during our pregnancies and 'compared notes'. We arranged to take the older children to the indoor soft play area, this was also the last place I remember Emily being alive. It was nice not to have to go there alone. I was so pleased my friend brought her new baby. I didn't know how I would react, but I wanted to deal with it, however it might make me feel. I felt I needed to warn Abigail about the new baby to help her cope, but that probably wasn't necessary as she took everything in her stride.

I looked at the new baby and I thought, 'That's not Emily.' I didn't feel any jealousy. I didn't want anyone else's baby; I wanted my own. I did feel sad, looking at my friend who had everything that I had been expecting. I had to keep reminding myself of God's promise of a hope and future for us. It was still good to be able to share our birth experiences. At least I had that.

Sometimes I would worry that other people would think I wanted their babies. I didn't want to appear over-enthusiastic in case they suddenly felt their baby was unsafe, in danger of being snatched away like the stories on the news or *The Hand that Rocks the Cradle*!

At night, we were trying not to take too many sleeping pills, as we didn't want to become addicted to them. So I would lie in bed and wait for sleep to come. One night I felt immensely sad, but I could not cry. The tears wouldn't come. Instead, I felt an ache in the middle of my chest: the very centre of my being hurt deep inside. It was a real physical pain. I was not alarmed as I didn't feel unwell. All I felt was sadness. This pain I could only describe as heartache; a manifestation of my grief. Sometimes I also found that the memories of what happened brought with them a wave of nausea and a heavy, gut wrenching feeling of dread.

We continued to read our Bible and go to church and I felt God spoke to me more. I was led to think that this time I now had was a time of opportunity. It was not a delay in my life, it was an opportunity to share how God helps when times are hard. The Bible says, '. . . and he determined the exact time set for them [people] and the exact places where they should live. God did this so that men would seek him and perhaps reach out for him and find him, though he is not far from each one of us. For in him we live and move and have our being.'[40] God had determined the exact time and the exact place where Emily had lived. Perhaps because of her short life and what we had learnt from it, others might understand that God does care about their suffering, that he sympathises with their pain and longs to carry them through and envelop them in his love. So I began to write my story.

Writing was also a way to express my emotion and grief. I could do this without dragging Tim through everything I was feeling. After all, he was trying to come to terms with Emily's death too. We were grieving at different rates now. Tim seemed to heal quicker and move on more easily than I did. At times I found this hard. It meant things became a little more difficult to discuss. There were times when I needed to talk, not just to anyone, but to him. So he persevered at listening, helped me along; a word of understanding and encouragement was sometimes all it took. Although we leaned on each other in this way and could help each other to understand what God seemed to be saying to us, it was only the words of God, in the Bible, that could truly answer our questions and lift us out of the dark places. Only God has that authority. It was his words and no one else's which could cut through the raging concerns and still my mind. For God is the only one who is all-knowing and all-powerful.

'For the word of God is living and active. Sharper than any double-edged sword, it penetrates even to dividing soul and spirit, joints and marrow; it judges the thoughts and attitudes of the heart.'[41] Writing my book caused me to delve into the Bible for answers to the questions that were in the back of my mind. I would think a lot about heaven. What would Emily be like? I searched through the concordance in my Bible and drew on my own knowledge that had been taught to me since I was a child.

'And they can no longer die; for *they are like the angels*.'[42]

Emily was like an angel and heaven was a whole different world, not like this one. Heaven sounded good, 'He will wipe every tear from their eyes. There will be no more death or mourning or crying or pain, for the old order of things has passed away.'[43] But this was talking about a new heaven and a new earth. So was Emily really there now, or did she have to wait until the end of the world when everything would be made new?

I turned to read the crucifixion of Jesus; as he was cru-
cified, the criminal at his side said, ' "Jesus, remember me
when you come into your kingdom."

'Jesus answered him, "I tell you the truth, *today* you
will be with me in paradise." '[44]

So there was no waiting, Emily was already in paradise. Oh, but she was so young, she understood so little,
could she really have got there?

'I tell you the truth, anyone who will not receive the
kingdom of God like a little child will never enter it.'[45]

As a child, she received it as a child, not doubting its
existence. She was really there.

But could she appreciate it at her age?

'And he [John the Baptist] will be filled with the Holy
Spirit even from birth.'[46]

Even babies on earth can know God and experience his
blessing, by having his Spirit living in them. Emily was in
heaven with God himself, so how much more was she
able to know him and experience his love and blessing.

My mother explained Emily's development in heaven
like this. A baby in this life is not fully developed, physically. Yet spiritual development is not dependent on
physical development. You may be fully developed physically without any spiritual awareness. Or you may be a
child who believes and receives God at a young age; your
intellectual understanding may be limited, but faith is
there – experience of God's love and forgiveness is there.
Or you may be old, your body and mind not functioning
as it once was, yet still be fully aware of the peace of God.
Spiritual development is based on how well we know
God. In heaven we will know God perfectly.

'Now we see but a poor reflection . . . then we shall see
face to face. Now I know in part; then I shall know fully,
even as I am fully known.'[47] So spiritual development,

knowing God, whatever age you are, is made complete in heaven. In the same way people will be complete, fully known in heaven. So Emily can appreciate all the joys of heaven, she can know God fully and be fully known. I needn't worry.

I would often find myself looking up at the sky, wondering what they're doing 'up there'. Eternity had suddenly become a very real part of my life. My focus had shifted. My life on earth now seemed so temporary. It was my workplace, not my home. One day I will finish my job here, I will leave behind its struggles to rest in paradise.

11

'THEY THINK IT'S ALL OVER'

❧❀❧

A s time went by many things touched my emotions, often catching me by surprise. I would think I was doing fine, that I was OK now, moving on; then suddenly I was in floods of tears. I read in a book that it would take a long time to get over my experience. This helped me to accept that this was part of me, part of who I was now and that it was OK to be like that.

There were still reminders everywhere I went. Some days they would affect me; even if I wasn't obviously sad, I would feel strained and worn out by the end of the day, often not having realised that grief had triggered my irritability; on other days they held no sway. The majority of reminders came thick and fast as my friends had their babies and other friends became pregnant. Having friends my age and friends with toddlers, meant that these things happened often. When I met up again with my friends, initially it could be a little awkward. People didn't know what to say. At times I felt apprehensive about these situations I had to face, about returning to groups or clubs, to the same places and people that I had enjoyed when I was pregnant. However, I felt I needed to face them sooner rather than later, before they became a

mountain rather than a molehill. A few times I did make
my excuses, but the times that 'I took the bull by the
horns' were never as bad as I imagined.

It was still hard watching when everyone else seemed
to be getting on with their lives. I felt left behind. At times
I still caught myself thinking that my life had stopped
while everyone else was still living theirs. It seemed like
they had forgotten what had happened to me, sometimes
I would think, 'They think it's all over.' I felt a little para-
noid, I felt that people tried to avoid the issue or worse
still ignore it; pretend that it hadn't happened. I thought
perhaps it wasn't important enough for them to discuss,
but in reality, people didn't talk about it because they
were distressed by it – they didn't know what to say and
they feared making me uncomfortable by mentioning it.
They didn't forget either; six months later I was still getting cards of sympathy and encouragement.

Often, if things were awkward, I would mention Emily
first. I loved to talk about my pregnancy, childbirth and
Emily. But I learnt that I needed to consider what others
were going through too. I needed to be sensitive as to
whether they were comfortable to talk about such things.
I found I could get so caught up in what had happened to
me, that I would omit to consider that others might have
had hard times as well.

As life continued I would meet new people and I found
myself dreading the question, 'How many children do
you have?' My heart would pound as I heard those words.
I had decided never to reply, 'Just the one,' as this didn't
seem quite right to me. I did once, just for simplicity. Then
I worried that I had not been straight. More often I would
say, 'We did have two, but our second died; she was stillborn.' Then I would worry that people would think I was
after sympathy or that they would think I was odd for

telling them so soon. So I couldn't win. Yet no one ever seemed offended by my telling them; instead it deepened friendships at an earlier stage. So I decided it was worth swallowing my pride; not worrying about what people thought of me and being honest from the start.

Being around babies so often felt strange too. At church there was a new baby, born a few days after Emily, and he started crying. I took Abigail out to Sunday school and watched as the dad tried to quieten him down. I felt so desperate to hold him close, but I was too embarrassed to ask.

Then often, when I was out and about and I saw mothers with their young babies, I wanted to tell them, 'I had one too.' Why did I want the world to know? I didn't understand.

Margaret gave me this analogy. She described what it was like meeting new people during the time she was apart from her boyfriend. She would feel like introducing herself, 'Hi, I'm Margaret, and I have a boyfriend. He's in France.' Fred was so much part of her and part of her life, that when people only knew her by herself, she felt incomplete. This was how it was with Emily. I didn't want people to look at our family of three and think that was all we were.

One evening Tim had gone out. I had been fine all day. I decided on an early night and got into bed. As I lay there, sleep evaded me; instead thoughts flooded my mind. I thought of Emily and cried and cried and cried. I felt so alone, no one was there to listen to me, to hold me tight. Weeks had passed; people had returned to their lives and now it seemed to hurt more than ever. Why was this? Time was supposed to heal the pain. Instead the memories cut into my healing wound more sharply. The intensity of the pain had increased, although its frequency had lessened. I was caught by surprise, and my defences were down. Would this grief ever go away? This enormous pain, would it ever ease? I was scared to let myself cry like this. I might never be able to stop. I prayed for comfort. Into my head came these words, '. . . weeping may remain for a night, but rejoicing comes in the morning.'[48]

Now I felt sure this sadness would end. I allowed myself to mourn, and waited.

Later I read from the Bible in the book of Job. I knew that Job had suffered much and his children had died; I thought it might be a comfort to me to read about it.

'Or why was I not hidden in the ground like a stillborn child, like an infant who never saw the light of day?'[49]

I didn't know the Bible mentioned stillborn babies. Job's life had been so hard that he wished he had never been born, that he had died in the womb. I rejoiced that Emily had what this man had wished for; she was in heaven and would never know any suffering.

I woke at a quarter to one and turned over. Tim was not there. He should have been back by now. Pubs close at eleven thirty; it might take him forty minutes to walk home. That made twelve twenty, so where was he? Fearful thoughts entered my head, 'He's been attacked; he's been run over and died!' Anxiety started to take over. I tried to get a grip and prayed for his safe arrival home. Then I heard his key in the door.

Why was I so panicked? It was the middle of the night, but even so I was overreacting. The emotional strain of the past events were taking their toll. They had left me much more vulnerable than I had realised.

Physically, it was not all over either. The midwives had discharged me, but I continued to bleed. It was Sunday evening and I began to bleed heavily.

'It must be a period,' I thought. I began to get cramps, like those I'd had in the days following Emily's birth. As the evening wore on the pain increased in severity.

'I've never had period pain like this before,' I said to Tim. I tried to sound controlled, to act normally. I had taken ibuprofen, but the pain was relentless. The bleeding got worse. Tim bathed Abigail and put her to bed. I was incapable of doing anything. Downstairs, I knelt over the beanbag clutching a hot water bottle to my stomach.

'I need pethidine,' I silently cried.

'It feels like I'm having another baby,' I told Tim. After about twenty minutes the pain became intermittent and a little easier to handle. I was able to walk around and managed to read Abigail her bedtime story, frequently changing my position as I tried to get more comfortable. I came out of the bathroom with Abigail's toothbrush in my hand. I stopped dead.

'Something's happening,' I cried. Tim rushed to my aid, white with anxiety. A large lump of placenta had been forced from my womb. The pain had gone, the bleeding was easing and I felt a whole lot better. Rather shaken, we phoned the doctor. Histology confirmed that it had been a whole lobe of placenta. I thought with annoyance, 'Why wasn't this avoided? Why wasn't this picked up at the time of Emily's birth? Or even from the postmortem examination?' But I thanked God that he had protected me from the severe infection that it might have caused.

Tuesday morning it seemed things were still unresolved. I dropped Abigail off with her cousin and sat and waited in the doctor's surgery. I waited an hour and then was referred to the hospital. There were no beds on the gynaecology ward so I had to go to be seen in casualty. I waited there several hours. I couldn't get hold of Tim. I was examined in a small room; left alone between visits. I listened to the groans and shouts of pain, from people in the adjoining rooms. I felt scared. I was a patient in this hospital again and I was all alone. I needed an ultrasound scan and then depending on the results, a 'D and C'. It was decided to try and get it all over within the day. So I avoided eating and drinking. That meant I needed a drip to prepare me for the scan. I dreaded the full bladder scan more than the operation!

Friends from my work at the hospital, arrived to take it in turns to come and sit with me. At two o'clock Tim finally arrived, having received the message that I was there. Everything was very slow. Sitting there was a reminder of our waiting for confirmation of Emily's death. It felt horrible. At four o'clock there was a bed available on the 'gynae' ward and soon after that I had my scan. That went well and showed that there were no further remains of the placenta in the uterus. The bleeding was put down to the possibility of an infection and I was sent home on antibiotics. It felt like I had wasted a whole day. An enormous palaver over nothing. It was just another thing we could have done without, but at least now our hospital memories were of something other than Emily's traumatic death and birth.

12

MY BIRTHDAY

❧

Monday 18th December; my birthday. Four weeks and two days since Emily's death. I turned a mere twenty-seven, but this year I really did feel old.

I opened my presents, Celtic silver earrings and a watch from Tim, 'sweeties, sweeties and more sweeties' from Abigail.

'You might share them with me, mightn't you,' she said hopefully as she helped pull the paper off.

Tall glass sundae dishes with deep blue handled spoons from my parents; a mud mask from my brother, 'Oh well, he always thought I was ugly!' I smiled – he wanted me to pamper myself; to relax and unwind.

We got up and had breakfast. Tim was off to work and I had the shopping to look forward to. I felt irritated. I'm not a Monday or a morning person at the best of times! And today, I couldn't shake off my feeling of anticlimax. I tried to make my new watch fit, but it slipped off my wrist and on to the floor. We had chosen it when I was pregnant and now it needed another link taking out. Everything seemed a source of frustration and I had the added pressure of, 'It's your birthday, you should be happy!' going through my head. I struggled through the morning with Abigail in the full swing of the 'terrible twos'; disobedient and unresponsive. I felt grateful when I could put her to bed in the afternoon. Mum phoned to wish me a happy birthday.

'Are you having a nice day?' she inquired.

'No, it's horrible,' I replied.

I cried down the phone for an hour, letting out all my frustration and sorrow. I also told Mum the concerns I had that were boiling up inside my head.

'It all began when I was reading Abigail one of her favourite Bible stories on Sunday morning,' I said. 'It was Jesus' ascension to heaven. I was struck by the words of the angels to the disciples, 'why do you stand here looking into the sky'[50] You see that made me think of visiting Emily's grave. I tried to understand if God was trying to tell me something. It felt like he was warning me not to wallow in my grief and freeing me to move on. He wasn't forbidding me to go to her grave.' I added, 'I think he was encouraging me to look forward, rather than live in the past.'

'Yes,' Mum replied, listening.

'Anyway I went to church on Sunday with this going round in my head. I couldn't concentrate on the sermon and so decided to look up the ascension of Jesus in my own Bible. Then I turned to the story of King David and Bathsheba that you had told me about, do you remember?' I didn't stop for an answer, 'I wanted to see how David stopped mourning the death of his baby and to see if God wanted to clarify things through this. But do you know what caught my eye?'

'What?'

'Well, it wasn't so much the sadness of David, but I began to wonder at the grief of Bathsheba – she was the mother, it was her baby that died; she probably found it a greater loss. It made me think, "How did she cope? How was she comforted?" And do you know what I read?' Again I didn't pause for a reply. 'I read this "Then David comforted his wife Bathsheba, and he went to her and lay with her. She gave birth to a son, and they named him Solomon."[51] I quoted the verse that had stuck fast in my memory. 'Mum,' I said, 'I think a big part of my healing will be when we have another baby. This has really made me think that it is right to have another one. It is exciting but I think I'm going to need even more convincing.' I continued to pour out my thoughts. 'I suppose years ago when infant mortality and stillbirth were much higher and there was no contraception, this was always naturally the next step. Well, I feel this is God's way for us too. He drew me to read this. You didn't tell me that bit was there in the story.'

'I know, I thought that if it was right for you and you felt led to look at that story, then God would show it to you himself,' Mum replied.

'Thanks, but I still have some doubts. It's really getting to me. You know how I've been struggling with Abigail recently; well, that's made me wonder. Do I really want to do this all over again? Will I be able to? Will I enjoy it? Am I a good enough mother?'

Mum gave me her motherly reassurance and then asked gently, 'Have you read your Bible today?'

'No, I was going to do it when you phoned.'

'Well, I'll say 'bye and let you get on then.'

'OK,' I said

Once I'd put the phone down I picked up my Bible and prayed. All I could manage was, 'Lord, you know how I'm feeling, please speak to me.'

My Bible readings were leading up to the Christmas

story and as I read the old familiar words, something new struck me and spoke into my heart.

'. . . Your wife Elizabeth will bear you a son, and you are to give him the name John. He will be a joy and delight to you, and many will rejoice because of his Birth . . .'[52]

'A joy and delight to me.' Those words stood out – they made me think that my next baby would be a joy and delight to me also. That answered my question clearly and I felt I needn't worry about my emotions at the present time.

'A son, does that mean anything for me?' I wondered. Then I read, 'After this his wife Elizabeth became pregnant . . . "The Lord has done this for me," she said. "In these days he has shown his favour and taken away my disgrace among the people."'[53] I thought, 'The Lord is going to allow me to conceive, he is going to do this for me too.'

Although rather unnecessarily perhaps, I also felt some social shame at what had happened. I felt different, an object of pity. Reading that God took away from Elizabeth what was considered in those days to be divine disgrace comforted me. I was getting more and more excited. I read further on and came to the account of the angel Gabriel speaking to Mary, ' "Even Elizabeth your relative is going to have a child in her old age, and she who was said to be barren is in her sixth month. For nothing is impossible with God."

' "I am the Lord's servant," Mary answered. "May it be to me as you have said."'[54]

Two things struck me here; firstly, nothing is impossible with God – that's encouraging to say the least! Any doubts of getting pregnant were dealt with by this sentence as I believe God was highlighting it personally for me at this time. Secondly, my attitude should be like that of Mary, 'May it be to me as you have said'; this was both applicable to the future, to the other children that God was wanting me to have – I was to accept these as gifts from him and not to worry if God was getting it right – it was also a good attitude for thinking back on Emily. It gave me more of the confidence and peace that allowed me to accept that God was in control.

I got up from reading my Bible; all the heaviness was gone. I felt excited and the day was bright now.

I began to look forward to the evening out we had planned and waited for Tim to come home. He arrived back home, arms laden with flowers.

'I thought all the others were dying,' he said. The endless flowers we had been given in sympathy had lasted well, but only a few held their heads up now.

We left promptly and went to The Retreat; we had never been there before, so it contained no memories of Emily. We found a little table tucked to the side of a roaring log fire. Tim and I snuggled together on the bench-like seat, while Abigail delved into the colouring pack she had been given when we had ordered our meals. I was bubbling over with excitement and shared quietly with Tim how I felt God had confirmed to me about another baby. He was excited too.

We enjoyed our meals and when Abigail became too tired to behave we headed home for my birthday cake. We were just putting the candles on when Tim's parents arrived to wish me a happy birthday. They joined in our little celebration and Abigail delayed her bedtime a bit longer. What had begun as a bad day, ended with happy memories and the hope of new joy to come.

13

CHRISTMAS AND NEW YEAR

❧

Christmas when I was a child was a day of presents, nice food, games and a brisk walk through Regent's Park, in the chilled December air. The uncontrollable excitement of waking up to a pile of presents at the foot of the bed is lost over the years. No longer do I wake when it's still dark, scramble around in my bed with my feet on the pillow and peer over the edge, staring for ages at the pretty wrappings, not wanting to even feel them, lest I spoil the surprise. No longer, when the big hand is on the twelve and the little hand on the seven, do David and I rush into my parent's room and clamber on to the bed, presents in tow. This excitement can now only be captured – in part – in the lives of our children. Oh, I like Christmas in other ways now, being the provider of that nice food, celebrating that God came to live with man through the birth of Jesus, so that heaven's door could be opened; I enjoy spending days staying with my parents and seeing Tim's family. This year, however, a black cloud was hovering overhead, tears were threatening to pour.

On Christmas morning Abigail crawled into our bed, unaware of what day it was.

'Happy Christmas,' Tim and I whispered to each other.

'What to do today, Mummy?' Abigail asked.

'We are going to feed the ducks,' I replied.

'Yey!' said Abigail joyfully.

'Shall we go and get breakfast?' I asked Abigail. When she had finished I looked at her and said, 'Abigail.'

'What?'

'It's Christmas today!'

'Huuuh? We can open our presents under the tree!' her voice came out in a high pitched squeal. Our Christmas had begun.

We had so much fun unwrapping our presents and starting on our innumerable amounts of chocolate. Abigail's glee as she pulled back the paper of each parcel was pure pleasure to watch. She was such a delight, grateful for everything, I observed sadly as she opened the toy pop-up toaster.

'That was supposed to have been from Emily,' I said to myself. Next she opened the doctor's set we had given her, she got out the doll, the blood pressure cuff and the stethoscope. She began to listen to the doll's tummy.

'I'm checking Emily in dolly's tummy,' she said excitedly, unaware of the tears forming in my eyes.

I put the turkey in the oven, having finished off its defrosting in the microwave; defrosting always takes so much longer than stated! Tim and Abigail set to work assembling her scooter from Grandma and Granddad and then we left to go and feed the ducks.

It was bitterly cold, but bright and sunny. We were having such a nice time together, which made me miss Emily even more. I wanted her here with us, enjoying our Christmas. Not that she needed Christmas in heaven, but even so, I missed her. Then I began to worry. 'What if she's missing me?' My day clouded over again. I was concerned, worried that she needed her mother's love. She was being loved by God, but not by me.

'Does that matter?' I wondered.

The ducks were hungry and Abigail enjoyed, as always, tossing the bread. It never quite reached the water, but the swans always waddled over for that little bit extra. We got cold standing around and I began to feel more and more agitated as I tried to work through these thoughts. As a result I began to lose patience with poor Abigail as she struggled to keep her scooter out of the mud. We decided to go home.

Abigail amused herself for ages with her new play dough and, once again, all was peaceful; well, on the outside anyway. Inside my head, it was turmoil! I called Tim into the steamed-up kitchen and fell into his arms, sobbing. I asked him all the questions that were going through my mind.

'Emily isn't sad,' he replied.

'We're just sad for us, I suppose,' I pondered, 'not for her.'

So perhaps I was being selfish in my grief. The more I thought, the more I realised that God was the creator of all love. The Bible says he is love. Our love for our children is only as a result of our being made in his image. If the love I have for Emily stems from God, this must mean that by being with God she is experiencing this parental, even maternal love and, unlike mine, it would be faultless. My sadness was only because I wasn't the provider of this love; it was not because she was lacking anything.

We enjoyed our Christmas dinner together and pulled crackers. Abigail had her afternoon nap and Tim and I spent a quiet afternoon together. We played Monopoly, watched television and ate a lot of Christmas pudding! It was a lovely afternoon, full of relaxed Christmas feeling. At teatime we went to Tim's parents and exchanged presents. Abigail enjoyed the added excitement of being with her cousins as well as having more things to unwrap! Later Tim and I enjoyed a romantic evening with only the fire and candles to give us light. We slowly danced to our favourite songs.

It felt good to have Christmas out of the way, a relief that we had got through it.

This year I was particularly looking forward to the New Year. It would be good to leave our events in 'last year'. Although only a change of date, just another tomorrow, the turn of the calendar would be a symbol of looking ahead, of new hope for what 2001 would bring.

In between Christmas and the New Year we took a trip to my parents'. Like everything else since Emily's death, returning to places we had been when I was pregnant brought with it great apprehension.

'How will I feel? The last time I did this Emily was in my tummy. The next time was going to be with her in my arms, now I have neither.'

We drove our usual route to Dorset. The hours passed slowly and I remembered feeling pregnant in each place we passed. As we drove through Salisbury I could feel a hollowness in my womb and an ache in my breasts.

We stayed at my parents' house for three nights, and as always I enjoyed the rest from cooking, housework and entertaining Abigail! She would wake up in the morning and, instead of coming to see us, she would go and find Grandma and Granddad. They would give her breakfast and take her out. We could lie in together.

In the evenings they would babysit so we could go out. Our first night we spread ourselves out in the back of our estate car, snacks to hand. We watched and listened to the waves lap the sand on Branksome Chine.

The next night we went out for a drink by the crackling log fire, at The Lamb's Green Inn.

Then, on Friday morning we awoke to Abigail's squeal of delight, 'Snow, snow, it's snowed!' Abigail had woken up and looked out of the window to find that everything was covered in a layer of white.

We all decided to go to Badbury Rings and as we drove the short distance we found the snow getting deeper. Everywhere was beautiful. We drove through tree-lined roads, every branch dazzled white in the bright sun. To our surprise we arrived to find everyone in deep snow, sledging down the hills.

'Oh, I wish we'd known, we could have brought a dustbin liner to use as a sledge.' I looked everywhere to find something suitable. I hurriedly emptied our chocolate wrappers and drink cans into the boot and stuffed the carrier bag into my pocket. We couldn't walk far. Abigail just wanted to make a snowman; we coaxed her a bit further and managed to build a little crumbling man. Her disappointment at being unable to make one from rolling an increasingly larger ball down a hill was only eased by Granddad producing two shiny pennies from his pocket for the snowman's eyes.

As we walked on up the hill, Tim suddenly became enthusiastic over my carrier bag. Placing it carefully at the top, he sat on it and sped down into the snow at the bottom. Abigail and I fought Tim for our turns. I became a child again, shrieking with delight. I was thoroughly exhilarated – it was the best time I'd had for a long while. We went home, cold, wet and very happy.

All too quickly our little holiday came to an end. On the way home I could feel my mood slump. It was back home again to all those memories of disappointment, to all those returning thoughts of nothing left to enjoy; nothing now to do. With the old routine to pick up, once more the gap in our lives intensified. It was at these times that I needed to hold on most to the hope of God providing us with a brighter future. This is what stopped me from sinking.

I woke up in my own bed and my teeth hurt.

'Oh no, not another trip to the dentist.' But it wasn't an infection, or a cavity. It would right itself given time. I had slept all night with clenched teeth again. I was learning to push my tongue against my front teeth so this wouldn't happen. I realised that while I was away I hadn't fallen asleep to, or woken up to, intrusive thoughts of Emily's death; I'd had a break. Now, back in our own house, our own bed, where it had all happened, my sleep became troubled again. For months I would often have the same type of dream. In it there was always someone whom I had to tell of Emily's death. Not that it particularly troubled me to do this, but that was what I would dream.

⁂

New Year's Eve, a party to go to and a looking forward to next year; a new start. As it got nearer I began to worry. I thought back to last year, when we were planning this pregnancy. When we thought that this time next year we would have a new bouncing baby. Will I cope with this party, with my pregnant friends? With my memories of what seems like a failed year?

The apprehension made me miserable, but when I arrived I began to relax and enjoy myself. We played games long into the night as the children settled down to sleep. Five little girls and two little boys bedded down upstairs. It was Abigail's first taste of a pyjama party and I enjoyed watching her excitement as if it were mine. With my spirit lightened, I felt hopeful at the joys to come and looked forward to seeing the promises God had given us being fulfilled; maybe even in this coming year. The champagne popped at twelve o'clock.

We woke and turned over in bed, 10.45 a.m. – what a lie in! Although we hadn't got home until 3 a.m., it had been our first night at home, by ourselves, undisturbed since Abigail was born. It did feel good!

We had breakfast and thought we'd better go and collect our daughter. After her lunch, she was so exhausted by the previous night's events that she slept soundly all afternoon.

The next day Tim was back at work. It would have been nice to have been able to leave the pain as well as the events in last year, but this wasn't so easy. Every place I returned to, every event I had to join in was still preceded by anxiety, 'What will it be like now things are different? How will I react? How will others react?' I continued to feel self conscious when I was around other new babies and pregnant mums. I would think others were watching how I would react. I realised, again, that grief, even subconsciously, is very draining. My trust in God's word, his early promise of, 'When you pass through the waters, I will be with you; and when you pass through the rivers, they will not sweep over you,'[55] was what I clung to for my sanity, especially at times when it felt like my mind and emotions were at war. These waters often felt like a very strong current, demanding all of my might and faith.

I had forgotten what it was like to have periods. Every few weeks I would slump into a depressed state and sheer exhaustion; I only felt better when I realised that it was premenstrual tension. Tim usually realised this long before me! My first period had me back at the doctor's surgery; I bled like I had never done before.

My excitement of things returning to normal so we could try immediately for another baby was somewhat quashed. It was, however, not as upsetting as it could have been. Amidst all the confirmation to have another baby had come a gentle quiet word, which I would have preferred to ignore, 'Wait.' The verse of the Bible which had first made me consider this kept coming back to me. It was the story of Simeon in Luke 2; the Holy Spirit had revealed to him that he would not die until he had seen the Messiah, and so he waited. When Jesus was taken to be circumcised, there he saw him.

'Now there was a man in Jerusalem called Simeon, who was righteous and devout. He was waiting for the consolation of Israel, and the Holy Spirit was upon him.'[56] The Bible reading notes emphasised that this waiting was not a waste of time, it was the right thing to do. Simeon's waiting was positive and hopeful, he was getting on with living a life devoted to God and the Holy Spirit was upon him. So much so that he was prompted by the Spirit to see God's answer at the right time.

'Moved by the Spirit he went into the temple courts.'[57] What is more, the notes explained, it wasn't easy waiting. Simeon was glad to be released from it, 'Sovereign Lord, as you have promised, you now dismiss your servant in peace.'[58]

I initially thought that God was just referring to the fact that because Emily had died we were having to wait for another child longer than we expected. Then I realised that he probably also meant not to try for our third child just yet. Waiting wouldn't be easy, but it would be the right thing to do and the timing would be right.

I had phoned the hospital to see why our appointment for Emily's postmortem results hadn't come through. I had been told it would take four to six weeks and it was beyond that now. What they told me was, 'Oh no, they have given you incorrect information, it is twelve to fourteen weeks before we get the results back.'

'Oh well,' I thought, God has promised us it won't happen again so we can go ahead anyway. We were planning to try after a normal period. Then I thought, 'Or was God really telling us to wait a little longer?' I believe he was very gently preparing me that the medical advice was also, 'Wait a few more months, until you hear from the postmortem.' So I was not upset on hearing this, but I just thought, 'That's what God said too.'

I went directly from the doctors to the family planning clinic, to arrange for more contraception. How hard it is at times to listen and obey God, but what a sense of freedom and hope it brought.

Everywhere I went I kept realising that babies grow up so quickly, time goes so fast, a year is nothing and when all Emily's peers are past babyhood I would still have a new baby to enjoy.

Although my periods were normal again, my emotional state around their time was not. Never before had I felt quite so despairing, quite so depressed and unable to cope with simple tasks. When I had a period it reminded me of my postnatal bleeding after having Emily. My life that had picked up and was so very full of exciting new things to do would become far too stressful. Everything I would enjoy the rest of the month lost its appeal. I would get irritated with both Abigail and Tim and think they were to blame. I began to learn to ease my timetable off at these times and to try very hard to be patient. It wasn't easy, in fact it was a hard struggle and one which I would

all too often fail at. Some days every little thing I had to
do was like climbing a huge mountain. I prayed for God's
Holy Spirit to keep filling me so that I could be patient
and kind and find some contentment. There was no way
I was succeeding trying to achieve this by myself. I knew
that God would help me change. I put my confidence in
his word which says, 'For it is *God who works in you* to will
and to act according to his good purpose.'[59]

As always the word of God held the key and had the
answer to all my struggles; God was showing himself to
be so gracious. If only I would listen to him more and not
let my own thoughts crowd him out. I also prayed that
God would heal me of this premenstrual depression. I said
to him, 'God, you know that I don't have the option of taking any drugs for this, as in a few months I might be pregnant. So God, please stabilise my hormones. I can't go on
like this.' I went from feeling so pent up that I could punch
holes in the walls, to a relative calm the next month. That
was a miracle and relief for the whole family.

Despite these difficulties, the New Year brought with it
many new things to enjoy. My writing continued to be a
great help to me and I felt it gave me a sense of purpose.
I began to do some voluntary reception work one afternoon a week for a counselling service. I sorted out their
little library, and being a dietitian I updated their healthy
eating information. Then, as Abigail went to preschool
more and more, I savoured the times we had together. We
got stuck into lots of art and crafts and learning together.
We started going swimming too. The first time, despite
her armbands, Abigail clung to me. Only towards the end
of the session did she relax enough to stretch out in the
water and just hold my hands. Eventually she swam the
length of the little pool, her bands holding her up, and she
slid confidently down the slide splashing into deep water.

Yet my greatest thrill was seeing her learn about and develop her own friendship with Jesus as we read Bible stories and prayed together.

Then I got a big surprise. A most romantic gesture from my kind, loving husband. I had been twiddling around on my friend's piano, finding that I quite enjoyed it. It was so much easier now than when I had given up after a term learning it at school. Perhaps learning to drive since had improved my co-ordination. My friend and I had joked and pointed out to Tim where there was a piano shaped space in our dining room and then I thought no more about it. Until, that is, one Saturday afternoon.

I had come back from taking Abigail to a party and Tim had returned from looking around the shops for a dining room table, or so I thought. In fact he had obviously spotted something else on his travels since he asked me if I would like another piece of furniture in the dining room. I immediately said no, I didn't think we needed an expensive Welsh dresser or whatever it was going to be. But Tim persisted until I was desperate to know what it was and then he told me he had chosen, with the help of Margaret, a second-hand piano. I was thrilled.

'I nearly missed it, didn't I?' I said jokingly. 'Like when you proposed.'

This had been when we had gone away for the weekend to a little shack in Dartmoor. Our only water had been the stream running by outside. Our only light was the sun by day and the moon by night, our warmth, a camp fire. We walked the moors, Tim heading for the top of Steepleton Tor. I knew that we would never get there, I was too tired. So, as Tim suggested, we sat down on a rock amongst the sheep. Tim was quiet, so I filled the stillness with chit-chat. He tried to interrupt me but I continued to talk. Eventually he managed to squeeze his proposal in, but he teased me saying that I had nearly missed it as I had been more interested in talking to the sheep!

Before Tim went to pay for the piano, we prayed and read the Bible together. We wanted to be sure it was right to spend our money this way.

That night, I could not sleep because of my excitement. I hadn't felt like this since I was a child at Christmas. I was so looking forward to my surprise, so animated by the recreation it would bring. So in love with my husband, so blessed by the gift of a new interest! What a joy it turned out to be. I bought piano books and tunes I had always loved. I found it a great vehicle for relieving tension, a wonderful way to relax. Just how music soothed King Saul: '. . . David would take his harp and play. Then relief would come to Saul; he would feel better . . .'[60] So the piano became a therapy for me. It was a wonderful way to come into God's presence too. My limited playing, often with just the top row of notes on one hand, was still a means of singing songs from church, which would reaffirm my faith and cause me to worship.

14

A HOLIDAY

❧

I awoke in the night from a dream; I had been dreaming about Emily. My arms felt heavy, I had held her. I could still feel the weight of her cradled against me. At times like this I would realise how deep the pain of grief runs, how long it continues to gnaw away, even when you think you're recovering.

For a long time I would wake up in the night, I would toss and turn, unable to get back to sleep. Day and night Emily's death was always before me. If I didn't wake in the night, I would wake up exhausted in the morning, feeling like I'd had no rest. At times I felt truly gutted, sick with disappointment. Death had left me feeling empty and vulnerable. Death is too ugly and pitiful to dwell on for long. These verses from the Bible helped me through these times.

'When I awake, I am still with you.'[61]

'I will ransom them from the power of the grave; I will redeem them from death. Where, O death, are your plagues? Where, O grave, is your destruction?'[62]

I felt the urge to return to the graveside, it was something I wanted to do, even if only out of curiosity. I put it off for a while, scared it would drag up all the sadness and undo the healing that had begun. The more I put it off, the more it became an issue, so I had to go and deal with it.

It was a sunny day, bitterly cold, but bright; the afternoon was ending and I was alone. I parked badly on the side of the road, obstructing an oncoming car. My thoughts were focused on what I was about to do. I bought some daffodils and then drove on into the cemetery to where Emily's grave was. There had been a lot of rain and I squelched through the thick mud. The flowers from months before were now just twigs, the bows grey and muddy. I pulled the old bows from the bouquets. They were cold and wet and my hands became sore and muddy, pricked by the dead rose thorns. I discarded the bows and wrappers, but let the twigs remain. I then placed the fresh, bright yellow daffodils individually on top of the grave. I sat on the fence and pulled from my bag the photos of Emily. As I looked through I felt undisturbed, but on reaching the one of Tim cradling her in his arms, I cried and cried. As I sat there and cried, I allowed myself to think of the body under the earth. My momentary desire was to dig her up and cuddle her. After all, was she any more dead now, than the last time I held her? As I sat and prayed, I remembered this, 'Do not be amazed at this, for a time is coming when all who are in their graves will hear his voice and come out – those who have done good will rise to live and those who have done evil will rise to be condemned.'[63] I realised that even Emily's body was not wasted. She will rise out of that grave one day, she will have a restored, resurrected body in the new heaven and earth. In a similar way to what happened when Jesus died.

'The tombs broke open and the bodies of many holy people who had died were raised to life. They came out of the tombs, and after Jesus' resurrection they went into the holy city and appeared to many people.'[64]

I got up and looked at the sun going down. I thanked God that Emily was not under the ground but in heaven with him and I returned to my car. I went home, the deep red sun setting in front of me as I drove down the hill.

The next day we went on holiday; we had planned a week's stay in Weymouth. This was close to my parents, and Abigail was going to spend the latter half of the week with them. I had been packing quite happily during the week when suddenly, I was reminded of all I had lost. Our holiday items were buried deep in the cupboard under the stairs, put away at the end of the summer. To get to them I pulled out Emily's pram and car seat – they were still waiting to be occupied.

'They are Emily's,' Abigail said.

'I know,' I replied, 'but she doesn't need them now, does she?'

'No, Mummy, she's in heaven. We'll go there when we die and we will see her. When we're very old, in a long time, when Daddy doesn't have to go to work and when Jesus tells us we can go. I won't need to take my toys because there is lots of fun there. . .'

'That's right,' I said. It had taken a lot of answering of questions over time for Abigail to come to this understanding.

We arrived at our holiday destination; we had had a good trip and were looking forward to the break and time together. It was a place we had never been to before, a place with no memories except the ones we were going to make.

We parked in the only space left and entered the little terraced cottage. The place was beautifully kept, clean and newly decorated. Tim unpacked the car, Abigail filled the fridge from the cool bag and I went upstairs to make the beds. There in our bedroom a heavy cloud came over me; in the corner of the room, opposite the bed, was a cot. It looked so new and cheerful. It looked so empty.

'Wouldn't it have been perfect to have been able to bring Emily here,' I thought – there was a place for her. There was space for her in our lives, space for her in our hearts, space for her in our family. Holiday time is a family time and it accentuated our loss. The family was incomplete. My heart ached. I needed to hold her. Instead, I found myself comforting Abigail at the times when she cried, just like I could have done if she was still a baby; I would hold her head against my shoulder and pat her back.

I was tired, I needed to unwind, but I had too much time for reflection. New questions began to plague my mind. I so needed to hold Emily; I had to find out if I really would see her again. Sure, she was in heaven and I was going there too, 'whoever believes in him shall not perish but have eternal life'[65] but would I be in the same part? After all, could there be different parts to heaven? Will I really be with her? Would I know her? Or is this idea of seeing your loved ones when you get there just an invention for comforting the grieving? Deep down I believed this idea, after all God said, 'It is not good for the man to be alone',[66] and he had made Eve, a companion for Adam. So I reasoned that it would be unlikely that we would be separate from our families. I also knew that whatever heaven was like, we would all be happy. So perhaps the issue wasn't really an issue after all. Yet it still nagged, I still wanted to know, I wanted proof and I seemed unable to find it by myself. Maybe I so desperately wanted to know I would be with her because I felt such a need to embrace her. Maybe it was the reality of my loss settling in. I just had to accept that I would never hold her again. It seemed so harsh, so final.

The days went by and we enjoyed ourselves. We were right by the sea and a few minutes walk from town. We did a lot of shopping. I used to love shopping but recently it had become a drag, it seemed like hard work; there was too much choice, too much stress – I just couldn't be bothered. I felt old and untrendy as I walked around. I didn't know what to buy. Then I came across some real bargains and thought it was worth trying them on. I liked how I looked.

This boost to my appearance put a spring in my step and gave me new confidence. I felt young again and with this was born a new desire to take life by the horns and enjoy it.

A few days later, we dropped Abigail off at my parents' house. We went to a Christian bookshop nearby. I needed to see what the book I was writing was competing with on the shelves. As I did my market research, I picked up another book off the shelf.

I'll Hold You In Heaven,[67] the title alone touched my most tender place. I stood there with tears in my eyes, hoping that no one would come around the corner and see me crying. I read the back of the book. Its content was based on the Bible; it said it wasn't a myth for the sorrowful, but the truth to set us free. I felt very excited; it sounded just what I needed. I stopped reading, not wanting to spoil the surprise. I would buy it, sit down later and read it properly, thoughtfully.

The next couple of days were fantastic. For the first time since Abigail had been born, Tim and I were enjoying some time together, alone. It was like being on honeymoon again. We were inseparable, so in love. One afternoon we sat enjoying a drink in the garden of The Pulpit, the sun was hot for February. We were at Portland Bill,

the lighthouse was ahead of us and the sea to either side.
A couple came in with a toddler who shouted his first
words to everyone, 'Dada, dada, dada, dadada.'
Suddenly I was thrown back into sadness; I thought.
'Emily will never get to say that, she won't be able to
speak.' I knew that it didn't matter – not where she was.
But still I mourned the fact that she never spoke to me.

Later on I turned to my new book. As I read, I looked
up in my Bible the passages mentioned. I had to check for
myself. Did his interpretation seem correct? I also had the
notes of my book beside me. I needed to start to proof
read it at some point. Now its use was to remind me
where the Bible verses I had included were. Flicking
through this I came to the page which included the words
from Emily's funeral: 'Some might say, "But Emily never
spoke to us." Well, not in an audible voice . . .' How
strange I should read this after what I had felt that afternoon. I turned to Jeremiah chapter 1. My new book had
referred to this as it tackled the question, what degree of
life does an unborn baby have? What is their spiritual
capacity? The Bible says, 'Before I formed you in the
womb I knew you, before you were born, I set you apart;
I appointed you as a prophet to the nations.'[68] The author
was explaining that this shows that just as God had a plan
for Jeremiah, he has a plan for every child, even before
they are born, and where there is a plan there is the pro-
vision to see it fulfilled. I decided to read on in Jeremiah,
'"Ah, Sovereign Lord," I [Jeremiah] said, "I do not know
how to speak; I am only a child." But the Lord said to me,
"Do not say, 'I am only a child.' You must go to everyone
I will send you to and say whatever I command you. Do
not be afraid of them, for I am with you and will rescue
you," declares the Lord.'[69] This made me sit up. It seemed
to be speaking right into my grief over my lack of

communication with Emily. I must not say of her, she did not know how to speak because she was only a child. God's plan and purpose for her life here was fulfilled. How she has affected our lives has, and I believe will, speak to many.

I read on in my new book and was greatly encouraged. John the Baptist leapt in the womb when he came into the presence of Jesus, unborn in Mary's womb. It could be thought that he was in fact announcing the arrival of Jesus, even as an unborn child, just as he would do so with intelligent speech thirty years later.

God is not harsh, he showed me that Emily's communication and purpose was not limited by an early death. I was bowled over by God's love for me. His totally specific answers. I realised that no matter what I struggle with, however big or small, God has the answers and wants to bring me comfort. Suffering in silence is not his way! That book helped to answer some of my other questions too.

Will I see Emily in heaven? Will I be with her? Yes, because King David said of his dead baby, 'I will go to him, but he will not return to me.'[70] I looked into this further, what exactly did it mean? The notes in my study Bible referred me on to Genesis 37:35. Here Jacob also says he will go down to meet his son in the grave. The Hebrew for the word grave is Sheol, which rather than the graveside is considered the realm of the dead, where departed spirits live until Judgement Day.

It took me a while to get my head round what this place is like, particularly since in the book of Job, Sheol is described like this: 'There the wicked cease from turmoil, and there the weary are at rest.'[71] I got confused at this point thinking, 'How can that be right when I know from the New Testament that the turmoil of the wicked won't cease? Surely they contradict each other.' Looking into the context of Job's description, I realised he said this when he was in turmoil, when *he* was weary and without rest; his suffering was so great that he felt death could only be better.

I understand it like this: Sheol or Hades, the waiting place before Judgement Day, is like the remand centre before a trial. It is not as bad as it could be once sentence has been given. It is perhaps even thought to be better than some trials of this life, but nevertheless it is certainly not a pleasant place. Yet because Jesus has now died and come back to life, those who know and love him are able to be cleansed from sin, and they can wait with the judge at his house. Not in remand, not in Hades, but with Jesus in Paradise.

Like many things in the Bible, the truth is clarified by the words of Jesus and God also prompted me to look up one of Jesus' parables, the parable of the rich man and Lazarus.[72] Here the sinful, rich man went to hell or Hades when he died and was in torment, separated from God, while the beggar, Lazarus, who was considered righteous in God's sight, went to Abraham's side. This clarified that immediately after death, before the final judgement, there is a difference between where those that are considered righteous go, '. . . not having a righteousness of my own that comes from the law, but that which is through faith in Christ . . .'[73] and where those who are not made good through Jesus go. It also showed me that people do meet up in heaven, which was the real question I had. This was confirmed even further where Jesus says, 'I say to you that many will come from the east and the west, and will take their places at the feast with Abraham, Isaac and Jacob in the kingdom of heaven.'[74]

I continued reading the book *I'll Hold You In Heaven*. It helped me to understand that I will recognise Emily, whether she has grown up or not. Just as the disciples recognised the heavenly bodies of Moses and Elijah, even though they had never even met them before!

'Two men, Moses and Elijah, appeared in glorious splendour, talking with Jesus . . . Peter said to him, "Master, it is good for us to be here. Let us put up three shelters – one for you, one for Moses and one for Elijah." (He did not know what he was saying.)'[75]

I don't know how old Emily will be when I see her in heaven. I don't think age has much relevance in heaven. Particularly when one considers that ageing leads to death and that in heaven there is no death. So I suspect in heaven there is no age. Also the heavenly concept of time is quite different, 'with the Lord a day is like a thousand years, and a thousand years are like a day.'[76]

What I do know is that, despite her age at her death, her potential has not been wasted. Not only in heaven is she fully developed spiritually, but the unique characteristics that make her Emily will also be fully developed in heaven too. The book explained this on the basis of these verses, 'My frame was not hidden from you when I was made in the secret place. When I was woven together in the depths of the earth, your eyes saw my unformed body. All the days ordained for me were written in your book before one of them came to be.'[77] So before we are even formed, God saw our unformed bodies; he knew what we would look like. From the moment of conception our genetic blueprint, our DNA that makes us uniquely us was there, just waiting to be expressed through growth and development. Emily died not fully grown, but God, knowing the expression of her genes, causes her to be whole and complete. After all, God is all about fullness and wholeness, not about wasting and wanting. Jesus said, 'I have come that they may have life, and have it to the full.'[78]

Not only will Emily's potential be fulfilled but she will also be perfect, with any genes for disease switched off. Her nurture after all is heaven! Not only will I see Emily again, not only will I be with her, but I will recognise her and I will know her fully.

Some time later, I came across this verse in the Bible, 'Eli would bless Elkanah and his wife, saying, "May the Lord give you children by this woman to take the place of the one she prayed for and gave to the Lord." Then they would go home. And the Lord was gracious to Hannah; she conceived and gave birth to three sons and two daughters. Meanwhile, the boy Samuel grew up in the presence of the Lord.'[79] I suddenly thought, 'Maybe that's what Emily is doing – she is growing up in the presence of the Lord.' I was encouraged again and excited by the hope of another child that this verse brought me.

The time we had on holiday meant that I had another set of questions answered, another time of searching done, so surely the worst was over, or was it?

15

MORE CHALLENGES TO FACE

❧❧❧

The next week I returned to work. Most of my work is looking after Abigail and being a home maker. But on Thursdays I take a break! I work as a dietitian at the local hospital. This helps me keep up to date with my profession and put my qualifications to good use. For some time I've been working mainly on the care of the elderly wards, treating malnutrition. A task, which, like any other, has its frustrations as well as its rewards.

Returning to work now, after an unusual three months maternity leave, had some differences. Firstly, I felt vulnerable. Everywhere I went I remembered the last time I was here, with Emily kicking inside. My own department is small and friendly; indeed they are friends rather than colleagues. They had been through Emily's death with me, offered support whenever they could, so returning here was not a problem. However, leaving the office to go to my wards meant I had to face many different people. People who didn't know me so well and who wouldn't have known what had happened.

'Hi, you're back soon, how's the little 'un?' As I explained, people didn't know what to say – they were stunned, shocked and sad. I was glad I was the one telling them. I wanted them to be able to see me standing there, coping. Shamefully, I think some of this was born of pride. Yet I did so want people to know how good God was in all this, that he wasn't to blame, but that he was helping me through. I worried sometimes what people were thinking because I wasn't crying and I worried what they were thinking when I was crying. It wasn't easy. Just being myself was by far the best way. Only when I was vulnerable were others honest too. I learnt to begin to think before I launched into talking about Emily.

'Why am I bringing this up again?' I would ask myself. 'Is what I am going to say helpful? Or am I just wanting attention?'

The Bible says, 'Do not let any unwholesome talk come out of your mouths, but only what is helpful for building others up according to their needs, that they may benefit those who listen.'[80] I have always struggled with talking too much and have to pray regularly like King David did, 'Set a guard over my mouth, O Lord; keep watch over the door of my lips.'[81]

One day at work, I dissolved into tears with every kind word and hug. I had taken my lunch break early and popped down the corridor to see my friend Margaret in the midwife unit. She'd just had her baby and little Alice was two days old. I couldn't wait to see them both. I walked down the corridor. I passed the double doors marked delivery suite; my heart was thumping. A lump had formed in my throat as I remembered all that had gone on behind those doors. I walked on down to the midwife unit past their delivery rooms.

'Oh, that's better, that's where I was in labour with Abigail,' I thought. The midwife and consultant maternity units are joined together by a short corridor between the two. The separating double doors were open, revealing the two large, white delivery suites on the right of the passage. In one, I had given birth to Abigail, in the other I had given birth to Emily. Oh, it was like being stabbed with a knife, my heart ached. Yet I had to look, I needed to face things as I had opportunity; a bump in the road was easier to deal with than seeing a mountain looming ever more insurmountable before me. I walked on through the bays, each bed occupied by a mother, complete with newborn at her side. Excited, joyful families milled around. I reached Margaret, the last bed on the right. We chatted and I admired Alice. All the time Margaret's eyes were searching mine.

'Are you all right about all this, how do you feel?' The question in both our minds was voiced.

'It feels so strange coming here. Walking past the delivery suite brings it all back.' We cried together at the sadness we both felt.

'Everyone is here with their babies and I bet they haven't even considered that some don't get theirs,' I said. 'I feel like telling them they're so lucky! I feel like telling them to appreciate their babies.'

'They do appreciate them,' Margaret replied, 'one lady was telling me she's had two miscarriages.'

'I know,' I replied. Miscarriage, although different to my experience, I have come to appreciate through the lives of others, is no less painful. Death is death, whenever and however it occurs, and is worthy of grief.

Margaret continued to be a comfort to me, to listen to my sobbing and my memories. Alice was asleep, but I so wanted to hold her, if anything, I *needed* to hold her, not knowing how it would make me feel.

'Emily had a lot of hair just like Alice, didn't she?' Margaret commented.

'Yes, yes she did, dark too.' I was so pleased Margaret had seen Emily's photos. It felt so good to hear Margaret acknowledge that Emily had been just as much a baby as Alice was. Oh, what a good friend I have.

Margaret lifted Alice out of the cot.

'Are you sure you want to hold her?' she asked.

'Yes, I do.' She placed Alice in my arms. As soon as I felt her weight, I noticed that she was heavier than Emily. I knew, of course, that she was heavier, but to notice the difference of one and a half pounds dramatically, was quite strange. I think if someone ever gave me a series of weights to hold, I would quite accurately be able to tell which was Emily's birth weight.

Alice was asleep and I sat there, enjoying holding her. I felt very pleased Margaret had her own baby, despite my personal sadness. I looked down at Alice's face. Alice was Alice, unique and beautiful. I did so wish she would open her eyes; looking at the closed lids was too heavy a reminder. Although she was wriggling around, my mind still screamed, 'Wake up, wake up!'

Abigail was still accepting Emily's death in her own way. Before Margaret's baby was born she said, 'Margaret's baby is in her tummy, and yours is in heaven.'

After Alice was born and they were coming over, I had omitted to include Alice's name, I just said, 'Fred and Margaret are coming this afternoon.' Abigail had asked, 'Where's Alice, has she gone to heaven?'

'No, no she's coming too,' I replied.

Sometimes as Abigail played with her dolls she said, 'When I'm older, when I'm married – are you married Mummy? Because you haven't got a baby any more? Well, when I'm bigger I'm going to have a baby.'

'Yes, I am still married, Abigail,' I said, 'and that will be nice, if you get married and have a baby when you're grown up.'

I expect many children talk dreamily of their adult life, but the times that Abigail mentioned having a baby made me think that she was looking ahead to her own child trying to compensate for the loss of her baby sister. It never entered her head that she might still get a sibling.

I believe God had clearly shown us it was right to have another baby. And we felt it was right to wait a few months.

It was the beginning of the year. One of the first Sundays in January. We were sitting in church. Two little sisters a few rows ahead caught my eye. They were twirling around and around together to the side of their seats, watching as their dresses billowed out. They laughed and played happily. Suddenly I felt sad for Abigail; her sister was gone. The children's story time that morning was about Abraham and Sarah and God's promise to give them a son. Suddenly these words seemed to speak very loudly and directly at me: 'This time next year . . . you will have a son.' I sat bolt upright, wondering if I dared believe this was for me. Or was I being silly, hearing what I thought I wanted to hear? It was not the only time I had thought we might have a boy. In fact when I was pregnant with Emily I was reading Abigail the Bible story of God giving Isaac and Rebekah twin boys. This and the times when I read of Abraham and Sarah's son left me feeling a little strange. It always

jumped out at me that they were given boys. Yet I knew
Emily was a little girl, I knew I wasn't having a son, so I
thought I must have got it wrong.

But I wondered at it again when one day, I was reading
in the Bible about the new heaven and the new earth, and
I read this: 'Before she goes into labour, she gives birth;
before the pains come upon her she delivers a son.'[82] It
came out of the blue, it was figurative speech about the
New Jerusalem, but I thought, 'Will our next child be a
boy? Will I have a pain-free labour?' A positive answer to
both those questions would be welcome, but only time
would tell if this was really from God or imagined. I
wasn't sure, it wasn't clear. Deep down I wanted the child
that God wanted to give me, whether boy or girl. Even so
it was very easy to set my heart on a boy anyway. Pain-
free labour I did take lightly, after all pain was pretty
much inevitable, it was the curse of women in this life.

Looking back over the years, I believe I have had reassurance about all my children. When I got pregnant with
Abigail, naturally I feared miscarriage, and as I prayed
and read the Bible, I was reassured to read this: 'Never
again will there be in it [the new world] an infant who
lives but a few days'.[83] At the time when I read this, having asked God to speak to me, I felt the impact of the
verse and felt it was applicable to my baby also and so I
trusted in it. Then when I was anxious and praying about
her birth, I read, 'Do you know when the mountain goats
give birth? Do you watch when the doe bears her fawn?
Do you count the months till they bear? Do you know the
time they give birth? They crouch down and bring forth
their young; their labour pains are ended.'[84] However, I
was never drawn to look at these verses with Emily. But
there was a verse that puzzled me in the back of my mind.
I read it at the time I was praying earnestly over my fear

of Emily's birth. It didn't jump out as starkly as others, and I felt unsure of its significance, but it was one I remembered: 'Do not be afraid, for I am with you; I will bring your children from the east . . .'[85] I didn't understand what this meant, why from the east? It seemed strange. Its clearest context refers to the reuniting of God's people and their returning to Israel, at different points in history. Yet did it mean anything for me? Why was it sticking out in my mind? I thought perhaps it meant that I was not to worry because God would bring my child, but I couldn't be certain. Obviously God didn't bring Emily safely to me, so I'd just assumed that I must have misunderstood, which is entirely possible, and left it at that for a while.

I believe that if something is important enough, then God will clarify it. It seems that he has since revealed what this verse meant for me. I've noticed that in Bible prophecies which may refer to the new heaven and earth, the east is significant. It is where God's glory will appear from: 'Then the man brought me to the gate facing east, and I saw the glory of the God of Israel coming from the east. His voice was like the roar of rushing waters, and the land was radiant with his glory.'[86] As I pondered this I thought, 'Emily is with God and when I meet God, he will bring her to me, from the east.' That verse made sense now. Just as the Bible says God will bring with Jesus, when he returns, those who have died with him: 'Brothers, we do not want you to be ignorant about those who fall asleep, or to grieve like the rest of men, who have no hope. We believe that Jesus died and rose again and so we believe that God will bring with Jesus those who have fallen asleep in him . . . For the Lord himself will come down from heaven, with a loud command, with the voice of the archangel and with the trumpet call of God, and the dead in Christ will rise first. After that, we who are still alive and are left will be caught up together with them in the clouds to meet the Lord in the air. And so we will be with the Lord for ever.'[87] These verses also confirmed the answer to my previous question about meeting up with others in heaven.

With the promise of God to give us another child in the forefront of our minds, we had an unexpected challenge. I was reading the Bible and praying about our family life and what God seemed to be saying was, 'I've given you the promises, now move forward in faith and take hold of them. Obey me and you will see them fulfilled.'

This came from a number of verses in Deuteronomy; firstly, 'Follow them [God's laws] so that you may live and *go in and take possession of the land that the Lord, the God of your fathers, is giving you.*'[88]

'See, I have taught you decrees and laws as the Lord my God commanded me, so that you may follow them in *the land you are entering to take possession of it.*'[89]

Just as the Promised Land was for the descendants of Moses to take possession of, so God's promise to us of another child, was what we were to take possession of, and the only way to do that was to get pregnant. I felt God was challenging us to enter into his promise now. It was the middle of the month, my fertile time, and there were still a few days to go before our appointment for the postmortem results.

'Shouldn't we wait until we've seen the consultant?' I wondered. Yet what difference would it make; we had waited the required recuperation time and whatever the results of the postmortem, we knew it would not happen again. But it was so difficult to take that step.

'What if I've heard wrong, what if it's not the right time and we get the wrong baby? What if it is the right time and we miss it?' All these things were going around in my head; so much so that it almost became too late. Tim's faith was stronger than mine, but I kept changing my mind. It was very frustrating for us both, but we went ahead and took a step of faith. I realised that my anxieties were not justified; God was a loving God, he was in control and knew that our motives were to obey him. He would honour that, all he wanted me to do was to trust him, and it was not easy.

Later on I still felt unsure. 'Did we do the right thing? Or should we have waited?' It was too late now. I turned to the Bible, in need of peace. I came across the testing of Abraham in Genesis chapter 22. God had asked him to sacrifice his son, his only son, through whom God had promised numerous descendants! How could that be right? Yet Abraham had clearly heard God's voice and trusted him, 'Abraham reasoned that God could raise the dead,'[90] so he was obedient and made preparations to sacrifice Isaac, even though it must have 'gone against the grain'. This is what happened:

> Then he reached out his hand and took the knife to slay his son. But the angel of the Lord called out to him from heaven, 'Abraham! Abraham!'
>
> 'Here I am,' he replied.
>
> 'Do not lay a hand on the boy,' he said. 'Do not do anything to him. Now I know that you fear God, because you have not withheld from me your son, your only son.'
>
> Abraham looked up and there in a thicket he saw a ram caught by its horns. He went over and took the ram and sacrificed it as a burnt offering instead of his son.[91]

As I read this account I felt that what God had asked us to do had also, in a much smaller way, been a test of our faith and I was pleased we had been obedient.

I turned to the Psalms as I often do when I need a little light reading and encouragement.

'I waited patiently for the Lord; he turned to me and heard my cry. He lifted me out of the slimy pit, out of the mud and mire; he set my feet on a rock and gave me a firm place to stand. He put a new song in my mouth, a hymn of praise to our God.'[92] As I read this, the 'waited patiently' struck me. I turned to Tim.

'I might not be pregnant through this, you know, I think we might still have to wait. I think God just wanted us to trust him, to put it all in his hands.' I continued to be encouraged that we had done the right thing as I continued my reading in Deuteronomy and saw that God was indeed moving his people on.

16

THE RESULTS

Sixteen weeks after Emily's death the long awaited appointment came. We knew that whatever the postmortem showed it would not, and in fact now could not, change any of God's plan or promise for the future. Why were we so nervous? Why was I anxious and jittery all day? Why did strange and troublesome thoughts play on my mind? Perhaps they were just a fear of the unknown. I read my Bible reading for the day, 'I am the Lord your God, who brought you out of Egypt, out of the land of slavery.'[93] This reminded me that he was bringing us out of our tragic circumstances. It is true this was the very last thing we had to deal with regarding Emily, and I was looking forward to it all being finally over. I met and prayed with Rachel before we went. She told me a story of a friend who had gone on to have another child despite the medical risks because they felt God had said it was right, and indeed that child was fine.

'That's exactly how we feel,' I told Rachel, 'whatever we're told, God's promise remains true.' I was now all geared up to hear the serious reason for Emily's death.

We didn't have to wait to see the consultant. We were ushered straight into his office, despite being a little early.

The room was small and stuffy, even though the window was open to let in the fresh air and sunshine. The consultant swung round from his typically old NHS desk and greeted us warmly. He was a broad man with sandy-coloured hair. He spoke with a soft Welsh accent and was sensitive and kind. He gave us all the time we needed and patiently answered my list of questions, without thinking any were silly. I think he found the whole experience as daunting as we did. He began by explaining how normal my pregnancy had been, how there was nothing out of the ordinary to have given cause for alarm. Then he went on to show that the postmortem had revealed a baby without blemish or defect and a perfectly normal, healthy placenta. All the blood tests done on the baby and I were clear. There was no fathomable cause. No one could tell us the reason why she had died.

This was seen as good news by many people; family were pleased that congenitally there was nothing wrong. The medics were pleased that it would not impede any further pregnancies, although very close monitoring with fortnightly scans and early delivery would be required. Tim was pleased that there would be less additional stress in the next pregnancy. Yet for me things were different. I'm sure that whatever we were told I would have reacted in some way, as is my nature. But I was not expecting the new emotion of overwhelming guilt and the older emotion of fresh grief!

I had asked the consultant many questions about things I could have done that could have been a cause.

'Firstly, it is not your fault, nothing that you have done,' he said.

It fell on deaf ears as I said to myself, 'Of course, he had to say that, what was done was done, no point letting a woman think she was to blame, however true or false, after all guilt has a very negative impact on people. Read

between the lines girl, if he tells you to avoid doing something next time, then surely that must have been the
cause!'

I drove home concentrating poorly on what I was
doing.

'You did it, you killed her, your own daughter, how
could you?' these thoughts screamed at me.

'We've dealt with all this,' Tim reassured me, 'we know
that nothing we could have done would have made any
difference, it was in God's control.'

I knew that, I understood that, I accepted that, but I
couldn't let it rest. She had to die by some physical means
and I did not want it to be me who had brought it to pass.
I know that anything that I could have done would have
been through an error of judgement or ignorance, not a
deliberate act, not out of murderous intent, so no accusa-
tion was justified; yet still I worried. Tim was a great help.

'If we were to blame, then God would have been angry
with us, wouldn't he? But he is not angry, look how he
has comforted and guided us; nothing has clouded our
relationship with him.'

I read through my Bible and Bible reading notes. They
were based around the Ten Commandments, obedience
and forgiveness. They also emphasised that 'the promised land' awaits and it was God who brought his people
through the 'desert'. While this was encouraging to know
that God was bringing us out into a better place, the bit
about obedience and forgiveness troubled me.

Had I not been obedient, had I ignored some of my
instincts, some old wives' tale, that I should have followed? Did I need forgiveness? These thoughts didn't
come gently, or kindly. They came with great troubling
force, they made me feel ill, they made me want to scream:
'No!' They made me want to run and hide. I would never

be able to face people again, not after what I had done. Even if God forgave me, I couldn't forgive myself.

Tim did not feel this was what God was saying at all and deep down I knew that God wasn't out to ruin me with guilt; that is not his way. The rest of the Bible testifies to that. It is important always to take each Bible verse in the context of the whole Bible. Otherwise our thoughts and Satan can get in the way and cause confusion. When Jesus was tempted in the desert (Matthew 4) Satan did this by quoting words from the Bible but Jesus, knowing God and knowing the context of his words, answered him quoting the Bible further. Indeed, as I prayed later on another Bible verse came to me: 'It is the Sovereign Lord who helps me. Who is he who will condemn me?'[94] That was it, I had tasted a feeling of condemnation, of doom; this was not from God. My experience of God is that he gently corrects; he doesn't condemn in this way: 'there is no condemnation for those who are in Christ Jesus, because through Christ Jesus the law of the Spirit of life set me free from the law of sin and death.'[95]

Indeed, look at how Jesus treated guilty people. A crowd brought to Jesus a woman who had been caught in the act of adultery, asking if they should stone her. Jesus said, 'If any one of you is without sin, let him be the first to throw a stone at her.'[96]

On hearing this, the crowd dispersed and Jesus turned to the woman.

'"Woman, where are they? Has no-one condemned you?"

"No-one, sir," she said.

"Then neither do I condemn you," Jesus declared. "Go now and leave your life of sin."'[97]

'For God did not send his Son into the world to condemn the world, but to save the world through him.

Whoever believes in him is not condemned, but whoever does not believe stands condemned already beause he has not believed in the name of God's one and only Son.'[98]

Earlier that day I had gone to a coffee morning and Bible study group, where we had looked at how Moses had prayed to God, how his attitude had been nothing short of demanding: 'Then Moses said, "Now show me your glory." '[99] Did God say, 'Who are you to talk to me like that?' Did he say, 'You sinner, what a terrible thing you have asked?' No, he said, ' "you cannot see my face, for no-one may see me and live." Then the Lord said, "There is a place near me where you may stand on a rock. When my glory passes by, I will put you in a cleft in the rock and cover you with my hand until I have passed by. Then I will remove my hand and you will see my back; but my face must not be seen." '[100] What a patient, considerate and sensitive heavenly Father we have.

It is Satan who condemns, who lies, who tempts us to believe him and his very name means 'accuser'. 'When he lies, he speaks his native language, for he is a liar and the father of lies.'[101] We must resist him: 'Be self-controlled and alert. Your enemy the devil prowls around like a roaring lion looking for someone to devour. Resist him, standing firm in the faith'.[102]

I had a chat with my own GP. He also helped me to see that it was nothing I had done that had caused Emily's death. Being a Christian too, I was able to talk to him about what God had been saying to me, that he wasn't condemning me. He encouraged me to hold on to these things in faith. Perhaps the verse that brought me most encouragement and freedom was this: 'All the days ordained for me were written in your book before one of them came to be.'[103] Even before conception God knew that Emily would be conceived and he knew that she would live exactly thirty-eight weeks. It was already determined and recorded, so nothing I could have done would have changed that.

So, if I wasn't responsible for her death, who was? Was God? No, God loves life, he created life. Yes, he did allow her death, he did give permission for it. Yet he didn't want Emily to die any more than we did, he mourned her loss too. He grieved with us in our pain and supported us each step of the way. Of course, in an ideal world she would not have died; in an ideal world, no one dies, and if we know Christ we will one day live in that world. But for now we are here, where humanity has turned its back on God, where humankind sins, and humanity is faced with the consequences, and so where Satan has been given (limited) power.

God decided that it was OK that Emily's life would be this short. I do not know why. Yet I do know that he is a loving God and he had his reason and that he will cause good to come from it. 'And we know that in all things God works for the good of those who love him'.[104] Whatever is OK by God is OK by me.

17

PREGNANT?

❧

Two weeks before my period was due, I could feel painful lumps in my breasts. I was waking up with headaches and felt exhausted.

'Oh, I'm pregnant, I must be pregnant, and maybe we don't have to wait after all.'

Excitement and joy filled me. Yet I had to wait another two weeks before I could be sure. Every so often I would feel my breasts to see if they were still tender. At times I was totally convinced I was pregnant while at other times I was less sure. A week later my period came. Oh, I was so disappointed, so sad. My premenstrual symptoms had been so deceiving. I was grateful my period was early – at least I hadn't gone through another week of rising hopes which would have been shattered with even greater intensity.

It was Mother's Day in a few days. This made things worse; I was so aware that I still only had one child with me. I went to choose a card for my mother and had to do so in a great hurry as I fought the tears welling up in my eyes. I got out of the shop quickly and took a deep breath.

It was so important to me this year that I was acknowledged as Emily's mum too. This past year I had been her

mother and it was the only year that I could be, so Tim
signed her name next to Abigail's, on my card.

My toddler group gave glass-like flowers to all the
mums as a Mother's Day present; whether it was inten-
tional or not I was given two; one pink and one white.

'One from Abigail and one from Emily,' I thought and
when I got home I cried a while; I was so pleased with
Emily's gift. Then I placed them both on top of the piano
and there they stayed.

I had the idea that waiting to get pregnant might only
be another couple of weeks, so we picked ourselves up
and tried again. I had got pregnant immediately with
Abigail; the first month we tried. It had taken four
months to get pregnant with Emily, but we hadn't tried
quite so hard! I was not expecting to wait long. My friend
tried to keep me on an even keel: 'Have you read that bit
in Ecclesiastes recently, "a time for everything . . . he
makes everything beautiful in its time"?'

'I have,' I replied, but later went to read it again: maybe
I'd missed something, or why would it seem God had
asked Margaret to tell me to read it?

There was something I hadn't noticed before, 'There is
a time . . . to heal'.[105] My grief needed to heal more before
I got pregnant. No, I didn't want to wait any more; I let
that verse slip to the back of my mind.

As the days went by and I continued each day to read
the Bible, God's words sustained and uplifted me. I
poured out to God my disappointment about not being
pregnant, I asked him why? I asked him when? This verse
stood out more than the others: 'Do not be afraid or dis-
couraged because of this vast army. For the battle is not
yours, but God's . . . You will not have to fight this battle.
Take up your positions; stand firm and see the deliver-
ance the Lord will give you.'[106] I thought about trying to

get pregnant: it did feel like a battle, a battle for peace of mind.

Was I pregnant or wasn't I pregnant? Yes I was, no I wasn't. These thoughts were not every few days, but several times a day and they felt like they were driving me mad. Then I read that verse; it's not my battle, it's up to God when I get pregnant. He will eventually bring it to pass and deliver me from this struggle. I just needed to leave it in God's hands. This gave me the overall impression that I might not get pregnant this month either. The very same verse was read in church the following Sunday, so I wasn't allowed to forget. I didn't forget, but again I pushed it to the back of my mind. It was easy to think, 'Did God really say that or have I heard him right? Maybe it was just my imagination?' I felt like this after I prayed for God to show me when I would get pregnant. I read this: 'The Israelites grieved for Moses in the plains of Moab thirty days, until the time of weeping and mourning was over.'[107] Thirty days, does that mean I will be pregnant or find out I'm pregnant in thirty days? Or is it just a false hope of mine and I'm reading too much into it? One thing I knew for sure; God was waiting until the time of grieving was over, just like he had said before, 'a time to heal'. I had only a little while until my period was due and again I had this inkling that I would be disappointed. As the days went by and I continued in my impatience I let circumstances be my guide. I began to lose focus of these things God was trying to tell me. I dwelt on the events and they screamed, 'You're pregnant!' as in the second half of this month, my cravings began; milky things, just like with Abigail and Emily. If I got too hungry I began to feel sick and indeed I was sick one night. I was tired and my breasts hurt. My menstrual cycles had been short and when my period didn't come after twenty-one days I was convinced I was pregnant. We began to get very excited. I lay in the bath. 'Hello down there,' I said to my flat stomach as I ran my hands over it. Then midday on Easter Saturday I saw a little blood.

'Oh, no!' My heart sank. I was taking Abigail to a party and had to try and keep myself together. Two pregnant Mums and a newborn baby shared my afternoon. It was all I could do to keep from crying. I still felt very sick which was only eased by eating a little.

'This has got to be wrong, I feel so pregnant, I've got morning sickness, how can this be?'

Then I realised that my period hadn't come properly after all. It was Easter Sunday. I bounded into church. How appropriate it seemed; a day for celebrating new life and victory over death and here I was, my concentration no longer on Emily's death, but on this new life inside. To be absolutely sure I needed to wait until Wednesday; day twenty-eight. Yet I could have told anyone who asked that I was pregnant, no doubt about it.

On Tuesday morning I woke to find I wasn't pregnant after all. It had all been a fantasy, my symptoms were so real that I just couldn't believe it. I was heartbroken. I felt like I'd lost my baby all over again. More expectations had been shattered. I sat around all morning, unable to do anything. I felt so depressed that I was completely useless. Tim was at home; by mid-morning he'd had enough.

'Let's go to Wales, we could go to see the sea, to Aberystwyth.' It was one of our favourite places to go.

'All right,' I said, but it was a long drive and was already nearly midday.

'What about Weston? It would only take an hour or so and then we would be at the sea.'

'Oh yes, that would be better.' Tim put some bread, a can of tuna and a packet of biscuits in a bag. I had a look and added some apples, but that was my only contribution. Tim bundled us into the car and we set off. I felt much brighter.

It was cold on the beach, but Abigail built sandcastles regardless. Then we went to the Sea Life Centre for a cup of tea. Abigail played in their soft play area. It was very crowded, it was half-term and everyone else was trying to stay out of the cold too. I hate crowds, I felt trapped and panicky. I looked at the family across the room. The little girl was Abigail's age and there was a baby in the mother's arms.

'Just what we wanted, just what we would have had.' My eyes filled with tears and I looked away. It hurt more now than it had in a long time, there was still no brother or sister for Abigail. I felt back to square one, mourning Emily all over again. Our family was so incomplete and I was achingly sad.

❧

B ack at work it hurt all over again too. I felt I was going nowhere. I began to feel everything was getting wasted. Those who had graduated after me were now in positions ahead of me. I had so willingly put aside my career for my family; with Abigail getting bigger and due to start play school, instead of planning the way ahead with my career I had spent that time concentrating on the new baby, coping with the strain of pregnancy, preparing Abigail and getting things ready; but now I had neither a flourishing career, nor a new baby. I remembered these

words in the book of Isaiah: 'But I said, "I have laboured
to no purpose; I have spent my strength in vain and for
nothing. Yet what is due to me is in the Lord's hand, and
my reward is with my God."'[108] I was reminded that my
growing and bearing Emily was not a waste; I had borne
a child who is alive and enjoying heaven. Without her conception she would not exist, but she does. The reward for
my labour, my literal labour, is with my God. I needed to
keep remembering all God's words of truth, of comfort
and hope that had brought me this far.

The next month we decided to be a little more proac-
tive in our pregnancy planning. Each morning I took my
temperature, looking for the drop and sudden rise that
indicated ovulation. It didn't seem very obvious, but at
least I felt I was doing all I could and leaving the rest to
God. I awoke one night feeling very irritable.

'Oh, no. I'm premenstrual again.' The next day I said,
'God, I cannot go through another month of these ups
and downs, I cannot go through such disappointment all
over again. If only I could be sure when I would be pregnant. Whether I am or not? Please, give me some more
answers. I need to be unshakably prepared this time.' I
was confused about that thirty days, that would be the
10th May, neither a day when I was likely to get pregnant
or a day when I would be likely to find out, so what did
it mean? Did God just mean next month or did he not
mean anything by it?

As I read the Bible I saw the deep cry of my heart
expressed there.

'From the ends of the earth I call to you, I call as my
heart grows faint; lead me to the rock that is higher than
I. For you have been my refuge, a strong tower against the
foe. I long to dwell in your tent for ever and take refuge
in the shelter of your wings. For you have heard my

vows, O God; you have given me the heritage of those who fear your name.'[109] God had been my strength and refuge through all my grief. He had heard me again and would continue to help. His promise of another child was unchanging; it was the gift I was waiting to receive from my Father. It was like my heritage. I did feel encouraged and I read on.

'They fully intend to topple him from his lofty place; they take delight in lies . . . Find rest, O my soul, in God alone; my hope comes from him. He alone is my rock and my salvation; he is my fortress, I shall not be shaken . . . Trust in him at all times, O people; pour out your hearts to him, for God is our refuge.'[110] As I read this I realised I was in a battle. Satan was out there trying to knock me down; after all the close encounters I had had with God, Satan was trying to muscle in, to push me to the ground, to crush me and tell me lies. Yet I could trust God to hold me tight and not let me be shaken. These verses made me feel that even though the struggle might not yet be over and I might still have to wait, now I felt a little more confident that I would cope regardless. At this time I began to get new ideas and interests in things I could be working on. There were new goals I could work towards and I felt happy. My confidence grew as I read more of the Psalms: 'Then my enemies will turn back when I call for help. By this I will know that God is for me.'[111] 'For you have delivered me from death *and my feet from stumbling*'.[112] 'They return at evening, snarling like dogs, and prowl around the city. They wander about for food but are not satisfied. But I will sing of your strength, in the morning I will sing of your love; for you are my fortress, my refuge in times of trouble.'[113] 'Give us aid against the enemy, for the help of man is worthless. With God we shall gain the victory, and he will trample down our enemies.'[114] 'O God you are my God, earnestly I seek you; my soul thirsts for you, my body longs for you, in a dry and weary land where there is no water . . . My soul will be satisfied as with the richest of foods . . . My soul clings to you; your right hand upholds me. . . . all who swear by [revere and trust] God's name will praise him, while the mouths of liars will be silenced.'[115] Even though my period (I also felt like this was my enemy!) might return and I was to face the same struggle as last month, this time I would stand firm, I wouldn't stumble and fall into depression and grief. I would be able to cling to God when all else looked bleak, I would be satisfied and sing. Satan's lies of, 'Look, you'll never have another baby,' would carry no weight. This time I was prepared for battle and I would overcome. I felt I was being led into action with new hopes and dreams and a fresh trust in God.

On Saturday my period started. I went to tell Tim.

'I feel a little disappointed, but I'm not devastated, in fact I still feel quite OK, looking forward to other things to do.' I sent a text message to my parents who were in Spain for six weeks: 'I'm not pregnant, but still happy just as I feel God told me I would be.'

Like the previous month, my period didn't continue and I started to get confused. Maybe I've misunderstood God. I re-read those psalms again. This time it was the message of victory that stood out more than anything. So perhaps I was pregnant after all. My breasts were not just tender; they were hard. Hang on, I was not going to go through the 'Am I? Aren't I?' routine. I read this in James 1:6–8: 'But when he asks, he must believe and not doubt, because he who doubts is like a wave of the sea, blown and tossed by the wind. That man should not think he will receive anything from the Lord; he is a double-mind-ed man, unstable in all he does.' My faith must not be so tossed by circumstances; I would leave it with God and wait and see, trusting that he would get me through.

Tuesday morning; still no proper period. It should have come by now. I did a pregnancy test and left it on the windowsill for the required three minutes. Tim went in to shave and locked the bathroom door.

'Where are the lines supposed to be if you're pregnant?'

'One in each little window.'

'Oh.'

'Why? What is it? Let me see!' The door remained firmly locked as I rattled it noisily.

'He's teasing me,' I thought, 'it must be positive.' Indeed it was and the line didn't fade even though I kept it for a week!

18

A NEW LIFE INSIDE

❦

'I t's often the way,' Margaret said to me. 'When you become content with what you've got, that's when God will give you the desires of your heart.'

Perhaps I had heard God right the first time. The thirty days, indicating next month, seemed to have been right; the message we'd had back in January, 'This time next year . . .' also seemed correct – this baby would be due in January! And when I thought my period had come I had withstood the disappointment and hadn't plunged back into the depths of grief. Was this the level of healing God had been waiting for? I was pregnant, the battle was won! Or was it?

Eight months is a long time to wait, especially when you've already had nine months of pregnancy and not brought your baby home. Yet now, I knew there were things I wanted to do in this time, so I was not as impatient as I might have been. I carried on blissfully for a few days and then I felt so very ill.

I hate feeling sick and I struggled with this, barely able to leave the house. I had in my mind that for some reason this pregnancy would be different. After all I'd been through I was hoping that everything would run smoothly and that I wouldn't be ill. I was cross. Why was I suffering again? I had the most severe migraine I'd had since adolescence. I was unable to speak coherently, the flashing lights and loss of sight persisted for four hours; the right-sided numbness kept returning to my legs, arms and face and the searing headache which lasted all night was only eased by vomiting. Although none of this was serious and really they were only minor problems, to me it just seemed unfair. Then I thought of Job in the Bible. He didn't suffer just once; he lost everything, his servants, his livestock, his property, his children and his health. Just because I lost Emily, that didn't mean that's the end of any kind of hardship and everything else will be easy. Life is not like that. But what I do know is that God will not let me go through more than I can bear; the waters will not sweep over me.

God was gracious to me; the sickness eased and that severe migraine wasn't repeated.

However what happened next gripped me with fear. I did not expect to react in this way. I was surprised by my lack of faith. I'd had more than my fair share of promises. I'd had a guarantee from God himself that this baby would not die. Many others had felt the same. Yet when the bleeding began, I was scared. The worry meant I couldn't concentrate and I was becoming increasingly irritable. Somewhere deep down I was trusting God and I knew it would be OK, but on the surface I let my mind wander from the truth; instead of focusing on his word, I was swayed by what I saw. It was only a little bit of blood every now and again and it wasn't unusual for me during my pregnancies, but it was enough to alarm me. Tim took over all the vacuuming, shopping and lifting of Abigail and I took it easy.

I kept rereading God's words to me. A while ago I had thought, 'God seems to have told other people that my next baby will live. I would like to hear it clearly for myself.' And I did. My Bible readings had lead me to the story of Noah and the flood; the rainbow that was a sign of God's covenant never to flood the entire earth again. I hadn't realised that the words were: 'Never again will all life be cut off . . .' These words cut so deeply into me and caused me to sob with joy. They so touched my spirit that I knew they were for my baby. And I felt sure this was for whatever stage of my baby's life, whether the beginning or end of the pregnancy. Yet I still needed more reassurance! A few days later when I saw the blood again I left Abigail to the television and went upstairs and sat down in the study.

'God,' I cried. 'Tell me again, so I know it's really true.' I felt a bit like a man in the Bible who could not believe what God had said to him and needed absolute proof.

Gideon replied, 'If now I have found favour in your eyes, give me a sign that it is really you talking to me' . . . Gideon said to God, 'If you will save Israel by my hand as you have promised – look, I will place a wool fleece on the threshing-floor. If there is dew only on the fleece and all the ground is dry, then I will know that you will save Israel by my hand, as you have said.' And that is what happened. Gideon rose early the next day; he squeezed the fleece and wrung out the dew – a bowlful of water.

Then Gideon said to God, 'Do not be angry with me. Let me make just one more request. Allow me one more test with the fleece. This time make the fleece dry and the ground covered with dew.' That night God did so. Only the fleece was dry; all the ground was covered with dew.[116]

God was patient with me also. I turned to the Psalms, laments that are complete in themselves and there it was, 'Lord you have assigned me my portion and my cup; you have made my lot secure. The boundary lines have fallen for me in pleasant places; surely I have a delightful inheritance . . . Therefore my heart is glad and my tongue rejoices; my body will also rest secure, because you will not abandon me to the grave . . .You have made known to me the path of life . . .'[117] This is what I felt; God had given me this baby, it was secure, it was my delightful gift from my heavenly Father. I could rejoice; my body, my cervix was secure. I needn't worry about miscarriage. This baby would not be abandoned to the grave, but would know the path of life. I went back downstairs and started on dinner. Tim came home. I shared the words with him and we both felt good. Whenever I had cause for concern I needed to consciously focus on God's promise, pull my thoughts away from things that might happen if there was no guarantee. It was hard; I cried tears of frustration, of exhaustion that there seemed to be no letting up.

I woke up with a cluster of spots that had been spreading up my leg over the last few days.

'Oh no, what are they?' If I was not pregnant I would not have given them a second thought, but now I wondered, 'What if it's something awful that will harm the baby? I know it won't die, but what if it's harmed in some way?'

I went to see the doctor. He was kind and understood my concern, but they were nothing to worry about. He checked everything to make sure. I went home. My mother-in-law phoned.

'Just think rainbows,' she said. I felt encouraged. Her faith was strengthening mine. I read again some verses I had pondered on a while ago: 'Their young thrive and

grow strong in the wilds; they leave and do not return.'[118]
A thriving, strong, independent child, that's what I'm
going to ask God for.

After about ten weeks of pregnancy things began to
settle down and life continued uneventfully for a while.

One day, as Abigail was talking to her granny, she said,
'There's another baby in Mummy's tummy.'

'Yes,' Barbara replied. 'You are going to have a little
brother or sister,'

'I've already got a sister.' Abigail said. Barbara was
quiet for a moment, waiting to hear what Abigail would
say next. Abigail continued, 'she's in heaven, but this
baby is going to come and live with us.'

⊷⊶

There were a lot of scans and checks. Each made me
a little nervous. Would I hear the heartbeat? Would
I see the baby moving? Yes, of course I would. I had to
learn to trust God. Perhaps with the same faith as Abigail,
which was simple and all believing, all trusting, all knowing. She did like to be reminded about Jesus' promise to
us. As she watched my tummy grow again she regularly
asked, 'Mummy, is the baby all right?'

'Yes,' I replied, 'and Jesus has promised we can keep her.'
The scans had told us to expect a little girl.

At first I felt a little put out by this. 'But I thought we
were going to have a boy.'

Even though no one else was quite so sure, I had
indeed convinced myself that this was what God had said
to me. I learnt an important lesson through this – namely
that I can sometimes misinterpret the words of the Bible,

making them fit in with what I want and my emotional state at the time. I can read them one-sidedly. So rather than feeling God had let me down, I had to accept that it was me who was wrong. I had 'misheard'. Dad took great pains to explain to me that while we hear God's voice clearly through the Bible about fundamental issues, such as the promise of eternal life through accepting Jesus, we can sometimes hear him less clearly when it comes to personal day-to-day issues. The fact that we are human and that we do not usually hear God in an audible voice means it is possible that we can get it wrong.

With these day-to-day issues, I think we need first to check that what we are hearing is consistent with what the rest of the Bible says. It also needs to be confirmed, perhaps we will hear the same thing in different ways at different times and perhaps others will feel the same too. For example, God's promise to us of a live baby was something that God had said to a lot of people at different times and in different ways, so this was not to be doubted. It was also necessary to pull us through another pregnancy. However, the idea of having a boy was something that I had read a little too much into, being swayed by my own wants. The first time I had the thought wasn't when I was particularly praying about it, nor did I immediately feel unquestionably sure that I had heard correctly – perhaps not like I have done at other times, when I've felt the power of God with me making his words very obviously relevant to me.

I now pray more that I would listen to God better, without my own agenda and without Satan interfering. It took me a while to gain my confidence back, but when I did I was much more at ease, not straining to hear unspoken words, but being a little more patient waiting for God's revelation. Thinking about this some more, I asked myself: what does God speak to us personally about through the

Bible and therefore what should we be expecting to hear? Guidance and direction is one obvious answer; the Bible says, 'Your word is a lamp to my feet and a light for my path';[119] 'The Lord will guide you always';[120] and 'I will guide him and restore comfort to him'.[121]

Comfort and peace are clearly brought to us in this way, as I've experienced many times. Hope for the future is too; we read of heaven, we read of God's sustaining love that causes us to trust him whatever life might bring. Yet is it really right to ask God to reveal our immediate future to us, for no other reason than curiosity or impatience? Is this not using him like a fortune-teller? Surely it's not always good for us to know more of the future than we need to. This patience is important if we are to avoid an emotional roller coaster of false hope. It also prevents us from having our security in outcomes and keeps our trust firmly rooted in God alone.

I looked forward to having another girl; I like 'girly' things myself and I thought a sister would be wonderful for Abigail. It would be as though all the previous hopes and plans could now be fulfilled. Abigail could look forward to a new sister, just like she had done before, and even those carefully put away summer baby dresses would be used – nothing would be wasted.

After much deliberation we decided on a name. I liked Amy, which means 'beloved' and was apt for the immense love I felt for her. We decided this would be her second name. Having two daughters both Miss A. Lycett did not seem a good idea. So we gave her the first name of Isabel, which comes from the name meaning 'oath of God' or 'God has sworn'. Naming her like this was a great help as during the anxious times that followed I could look down at my tummy and think, 'You're going to be fine, you're Isabel, you're God's promise.'

19

A LONG NINE MONTHS

I t was Thursday night. I was now coming up to twenty-six weeks pregnant. I had had an exhausting day working and we decided to choose a video to watch for the evening. Tim helped me get Abigail ready for bed as I could hardly climb the stairs. We bundled Abigail into her pyjamas, into the car and drove round to the video shop. As we looked around I realised that I couldn't stand any longer, so hurriedly we grabbed a film, some fizzy dinosaur shaped sweets and went home.

With Abigail now tucked up in bed we settled comfortably on the sofa and I put my feet up. The film had been on for a little while and I found myself unable to concentrate on it properly. I had felt Braxton Hicks contractions for a few weeks, but now I was developing pain that I could only describe as early labour. I had felt it before first with Abigail and then with Emily. The tightening began in the same spot at the top of my womb, and then it moved down bringing a wave of nausea with it.

'Oh no, oh no, oh no,' I cried, 'what's happening? God, you promised, remember?' I could feel our daughter kick and move around. I felt reassured. I knew she was alive. I knew she wouldn't die, but I was scared. It all seemed a little too familiar.

'I don't want her yet, God, not at twenty-six weeks. Please Lord, she's not ready.'

I tried to relax and finish watching the film. Later we went to bed, but I couldn't sleep, my tummy kept hardening. It felt like a solid ball beneath my hand. I woke Tim up.

'It really feels like I'm going into labour,' I said. 'I think we should call the doctor.' I was told a doctor would see me at the Primary Care Centre, but to be prepared in case I needed to be admitted. We rang Tim's parents and his mum came over to watch Abigail. She could sleep in the spare bed. Hastily I stuffed my pocket-sized Bible into my bag, along with my toothbrush and nightie.

At the hospital, I was told everything was fine.

'So she's not getting ready to be born?' I asked.

'No,' he replied, 'but you're very anxious, I'll send you over to the labour ward and they can have a look at you.'

'OK,' I said.

We walked back on to that same ward. Each time the baby kicked I felt reassured, but I was still in pain and feeling very ill. Tim left me to the doctors. The stress was taking its toll on him. After they checked the baby and me, I was reassured that all was fine. I wasn't going into labour, but they would keep an eye on me and give me a bed for the night.

Tim went home. I couldn't sleep; I hated being on a ward without any privacy. I drew the curtains around my bed and turned on the nightlight. I tried to read but I couldn't take my mind off the continual contractions. Finally morning came, but I felt no different, no better. Behind my curtains, I opened my pocket Bible. I turned to the Psalms and as I read through some of them, I came across this: 'The Lord will sustain him on his sick-bed and restore him from his bed of illness.'[122]

I felt reassured and full of hope. It was as though God was saying to me, firstly that he would help me cope with staying in hospital and sustain me, and secondly that I would get better, I would be restored. I felt that this meant that I would return to normal pregnancy. I hung on to this through the day. Tim and Abigail came and went. Tim came again on his own and sat with me as the hours passed. In the evening Margaret came and brought some books for me. She looked concerned as she watched me struggle to deal with the pain. As the doctors did their last rounds of the day I said to them, 'Why won't these pains stop?'

'They still haven't settled?'

'No.'

One of the doctors felt my tummy as it hardened and did another examination.

'I'll give you some pethidine and some steroids to mature the baby's lungs, then, should she come early, it will help her breathing.'

'OK.' I said.

'It doesn't look like it's on its way,' she reassured me, 'we don't need to book you a bed in Birmingham at the moment, we'll just keep an eye on things.' The baby would have to be born in Birmingham if it did come this early, as they have the special baby care unit that she would need.

The pethidine started to take effect and I began to relax and fell asleep. I woke feeling a thousand times better. I was a little high from the pethidine and the contractions had eased; they were still frequent, but much less painful. Every day that passed I counted as baby being one day older, one day stronger and one day more ready to be born. After another few days the pains had gone and things settled down, but I had to rest. Hugely relieved and immensely grateful to God for my healthy baby, still growing inside, I went home. The next morning my breasts were full of milk and nobody knew why. Perhaps my hormones had thought she was coming. I thank God for the miracle that she didn't.

Throughout the rest of my pregnancy I had strong Braxton Hicks contractions, but these were not accompanied by pain. I had a growth scan every two weeks and was reassured by good growth which seemed to rocket after the steroid injection I had had during my admission. Rachel took over my ironing and Tim helped a lot around the house so that I could rest more. He was off from work for some time on account of stress and depression. We had to trust God, we held on to his promise of a live baby, yet sometimes we could feel our grip loosen. Sometimes when she was asleep in the womb and I couldn't feel her kicking I would panic. I would pray, 'Lord, make her kick.'

As I waited and trusted I would feel her move again, but I'm sure without that promise I would have gone frequently, perhaps even daily, to the hospital to have her checked out. Even so, I found it overwhelmingly stressful. Any change or reduction in the baby's movements and I was supposed to go straight to the labour ward. It was like living on a knife-edge. Both Tim and I found that as the birth approached we became more and more strained and all we wanted was for the waiting to be over. On top of that, sometimes feeling baby move just served as a reminder of that time when I waited and waited for the next kick, but all was quiet.

um and Dad arrived on Sunday night. I had busied myself making a beef casserole, but thought I was unlikely to eat any of it. Tomorrow was the day. I was again exactly thirty-eight weeks pregnant. I was to go in at eight in the morning and be induced. I was very scared. Scared of pain, scared of sickness, scared of complications, scared that there wouldn't be a bed available, scared that it would all just take too long, scared that Tim would find it all too much. Two of my friends had come over and prayed with me in the afternoon. They had told God all these concerns and now it was up to me to leave it in his hands.

I remembered a while ago, when I was feeling anxious, counting baby's kicks, I had thought of the Bible reading for that morning. It was about God's covenant, not only the promises he has made to us, but also those we make to him. I promised God then that I would trust him more, or at least try. I didn't feel able to promise that I wouldn't be anxious again, but I was able to say, 'Next time I doubt, I will not only remember your promise to me, but I will remember mine to you and try to stop thinking that way.'

I would stop that downward spiral of anxiety that begins with 'what if?' and ends with a real fear of an imagined calamity, which in all likelihood will not happen.

We went to bed late, but I couldn't sleep – a total of two hours was probably all I managed. I was going to take a sleeping pill, but then had thought that if it made baby sleepier I would worry that she was moving less. So I did without. I lay there and felt the Braxton Hicks a little more than usual. Finally at half past six, I got up and had time to gather myself before anyone else stirred. I think now my nerves had been overshadowed by the immense excitement that I would soon have my baby.

I was induced at 9.45 a.m. I sent Tim into town to relax and have some coffee, while we waited for it to take effect. I prayed and prayed that it would be quick. By noon the Braxton Hicks were getting stronger and a little painful. I went for a wander around the hospital and dropped in to see my colleagues. Tim came back, but his tension was making me tense too, so Rachel came to visit and Tim disappeared for another hour. It was all very much nicer than I imagined; seeing friends helped me to relax, and having spent time in this antenatal ward a couple of months ago, I felt quite at home. Tim returned just as my waters broke with a huge gush. By now I had my tens machine (which stimulates nerves to produce the body's natural painkillers, endorphins) so high that at each contraction I sent what seemed like an electric shock vibrating through me; this jarred me sufficiently to distract me from the pain – for a little while at least! Rachel left and Tim and I walked into the delivery suite.

I sabel Amy Lycett was born on the 7th January 2002 at 6.20 p.m. She weighed 6 lb 15½ oz. She did not cry. She had slept through an uneventful labour and her first breath was a snore! My joy, my delight, my relief was indescribable.

'The Lord is faithful to all his promises.'[123]

Not only was my heart thrilled with Isabel, but also with Abigail's reaction to her. She was as thrilled as we were and could hardly believe she finally had a sister. She helped me bath Isabel on the ward and then settled comfortably beside the cot and read her storybooks. She held the pages wide open so Isabel could see the pictures if she wished and then being unable to really read she told her the stories from memory. Her love and care of Isabel continues to blossom, but she never forgets Emily. She talked of her often, especially when Isabel was born. In fact Isabel reminded us all of Emily. When she first arrived we looked at her and thought, 'She looks just like Emily.' She was a little bigger, a little plumper, but otherwise virtually identical. In the weeks that followed I often looked at Isabel asleep in her cot and saw Emily. Loving Isabel immensely, enjoying such a good and delightful baby initially made me sad again that I had missed out on all Emily's babyhood. As I read the Bible, God comforted me all over again and reminded me of the wonderful life Emily now lives and this wonderful life we have to come. Isabel now reminds me a lot of Abigail as a baby. We are living as that family of four that we all longed to be; God has restored that to us and our pain has eased tremendously. We feel complete, for now, with two children on earth, and one in heaven.

EPILOGUE

 ear Reader

I was brought up in a Christian home, my father being a Baptist church minister. I have had the privilege of spiritual teaching throughout my life. At the age of four, I knelt by my bed and asked my mother if I, too, could tell Jesus I was sorry for the naughty things I had done and ask Jesus to come into my heart. I still clearly remember the moment; I remember the little bedroom in Spain; the morning sun shining through the window.

As I grew up my understanding grew and my relationship with Jesus deepened. I remember sitting at the back of our little church in London, listening to my dad preaching, 'Is there anything God might be asking you to do?'

'Yes,' I thought, 'I haven't been baptised; I must get baptised.' So at the age of seven I was baptised. (Baby dedication, and baptism by full immersion when older, rather than christening and confirmation, is the custom in a Baptist church.)

At the age of seventeen I went away for two weeks in the summer. I formed part of a team helping a church to reach out to its local community. During this time, living

closely with my peers, I began to realise there were things
I didn't like about myself. Attitudes that were wrong, that
were stifling me and stopping me being free. I would look
at others with intense jealousy and wish I was like them.
I would watch the other girls and envy their figures, their
confidence and their popularity. Basically I felt horrible
inside.

I asked one of the leaders to pray with me, 'Just
because I'm so horrible.' As she prayed I had the most
incredible experience. I was kneeling on the floor, my
eyes shut and there I saw him. A vision of Jesus on the
cross; my view was from a distance. I could see his sil-
houette on top of a hill. He was not facing me, I was looking at him from the side.

'I did this for you, for your jealousy, for your pride, so
that you can be forgiven and free from it.' I stopped crying and just listened as these words filled my mind.

'Jesus, I'm sorry. Here's my life, it's yours. I will do anything for you.' From that moment on, all that I had learnt
about God in my mind entered my heart with new understanding. I was so grateful for what Jesus had done for me.
I understood my sin and my need of his loving sacrifice in
a way I had never done before. My relationship with Jesus
deepened further as I experienced him more.

God's Son did not die just to bring me liberation from
my sin. He died for every single person on the earth to
give them the same freedom, no matter what they have
done, to take away the guilt and punishment that would
otherwise be due to them. This means that everyone can
live in a loving relationship with a holy and just God.
Everyone can experience God's closeness, his guidance
and comfort when times are good and when times are
hard. They can rest secure that he has a plan for their lives
and he is in control.

This has been my experience of God. If you have been affected in any way by what you have read in this book, if you or someone you know has suffered a similar bereavement or if you are just interested in knowing God better, then please visit my website:
 www.stillborn.org.uk.

Debs

'I have told you these things, so that in me you may have peace. In this world you will have trouble. But take heart! I have overcome the world.'[124]

USEFUL CONTACTS

I f you have been affected in any way by what you have read in this book, if you or someone you know has suffered a similar bereavement or if you are just interested in knowing God better then you may find the following contacts useful.

Organisations offering help and support:

Bereaved Parents Network: Care for the Family, PO Box 488 Cardiff, CF15 7YY. T: (029) 2081 0800. F: (029) 2081 4089. E-mail@cff.org.uk. www.care-for-the-family.org.uk

CARE Centres Network (deal with issues of pregnancy crisis and loss), 1 Winton Square, Basingstoke, Hants, RG21 8EN. Helpline: 0800 028 2228. www.pregnancy.org.uk

SANDS (Stillbirth and Neonatal Death Society), 28 Portland Place, London, W1B 1LY. Helpline: 020 7436 5881. Fax: 020 7436 3715. E-mail: support@uk-sands.org. www.uk-sands.org

To find a local church: Find a Church, PO Box 364, High Wycombe, HP15 7XX. Tel: 01494 718773.
Email: helpdesk@findachurch.co.uk. www.findachurch.co.uk

REFERENCES

[1] Jesus meant permanently dead. As in the death of Lazarus, Jesus had been speaking of his death, but his disciples thought he meant natural sleep. See John 11:13

[2] Luke 8:51-55a

[3] Isaiah 43:2

[4] Mark 14:34a

[5] Luke 22:41–44

[6] Deuteronomy 30:20b

[7] Daniel 1:15

[8] Psalm 84

[9] Psalm 127:3

[10] Jeremiah 29:11

[11] Daniel 3:24,25

[12] Daniel 3:27b

[13] Daniel 3:17,18

[14] James 5:14,15a

[15] Isaiah 61:3

[16] Daniel 4:35

[17] Daniel 4:37

[18] Isaiah 55:8,9

[19] Acts 2:23

[20] Daniel 5:5,6

[21] 1 Peter 5:10

[22] Psalm 31:9,14,15a

[23] Ecclesiastes 3:1,2,4,11a

[24] *Living with Loss*, SGM International, London

[25] Matthew 10:29-31

[26] John 21:21,22 – author's emphasis

[27] 1 John 1:9

[28] Philippians 4:19

[29] 'The Lord's My Shepherd', Jessie Seymour Irvine 1836–1887 – author's emphasis

[30] 'Faithful One', Brian Doerksen. Copyright © 1989 Mercy/Vineyard publishing. Administered by Copycare, PO Box 77, Hailsham, BN27 3EF, UK. music@copycare.com Used by permission.

[31] Martin Hodson, used by permission

[32] 'There is a Redeemer', Melody Green. Copyright © 1984, Ears to Hear Music/Birdwing Music/BMG Songs Inc./EMI Christian Music Publishing. Administered by Copycare, PO Box 77 Hailsham, BN27 3EF, UK. music@copycare.com Used by permission.

[33] Philippians 4:6,7 – author's emphasis

[34] 2 Timothy 4:5

[35] Acts 2:44,45 – author's emphasis

[36] John 14:2-4

[37] 1 Samuel 1:27,28

[38] 1 Corinthians 13:4–8a

[39] 1 John 1:7

[40] Acts 17:26–28

[41] Hebrews 4:12

[42] Luke 20:36a – author's emphasis

[43] Revelation 21:4

[44] Luke 23:42,43 – author's emphasis

[45] Luke 18:17

[46] Luke 1:15b

[47] 1 Corinthians 13:12
[48] Psalm 30:5b
[49] Job 3:16
[50] Acts 1:11a
[51] 2 Samuel 12:24
[52] Luke 1:13b–14
[53] Luke 1:24,26
[54] Luke 1:36–38
[55] Isaiah 43:2
[56] Luke 2:25
[57] Luke 2:27a
[58] Luke 2:29
[59] Philippians 2:13 – author's emphasis
[60] 1 Samuel 16:23
[61] Psalm 139:18b
[62] Hosea 13:14
[63] John 5:28,29
[64] Matthew 27:52,53
[65] John 3:16
[66] Genesis 2:18a
[67] Hayford, Jack W., *I'll Hold You In Heaven* (Regal Books, California, USA 1990)
[68] Jeremiah 1:5
[69] Jeremiah 1:6–8
[70] 2 Samuel 12:23b
[71] Job 3:17
[72] Luke 16:19–31
[73] Philippians 3:9
[74] Matthew 8:11
[75] Luke 9:30,31,33
[76] 2 Peter 3:8
[77] Psalm 139:15,16
[78] John 10:10b
[79] 1 Samuel 2:20,21

[80] Ephesians 4:29
[81] Psalm 141:3
[82] Isaiah 66:7
[83] Isaiah 65:20
[84] Job 39:1–3
[85] Isaiah 43:5
[86] Ezekiel 43:1,2
[87] 1 Thessalonians 4:13,14,16–17
[88] Deuteronomy 4:1 – author's emphasis
[89] Deuteronomy 4:5 – author's emphasis
[90] Hebrews 11:19a
[91] Genesis 22:10–13
[92] Psalm 40:1–3a
[93] Deuteronomy 5:6
[94] Isaiah 50:9
[95] Romans 8:1,2. Cited in P. Vredevelt, *Empty Arms* (Kingsway, Eastbourne, 1988)
[96] John 8:7b
[97] John 8:10b,11
[98] John 3: 17–18
[99] Exodus 33:18
[100] Exodus 33:20–23
[101] John 8:44b
[102] 1 Peter 5:8,9a
[103] Psalm 139:16b
[104] Romans 8:28
[105] Ecclesiastes 3:3
[106] 2 Chronicles 20:15b,17a
[107] Deuteronomy 34:8
[108] Isaiah 49:4
[109] Psalm 61:2–5
[110] Psalm 62:4–8
[111] Psalm 56:9
[112] Psalm 56:13 – author's emphasis

[113] Psalm 59:14–16
[114] Psalm 60:11,12
[115] Psalm 63:1,5a,8,11
[116] Judges 6:17,36–40
[117] Psalm 16:5,6,9,10b,11a
[118] Job 39:4
[119] Psalm 119:105
[120] Isaiah 58:11
[121] Isaiah 57:18
[122] Psalm 41:3
[123] Psalm 145:13
[124] John 16:33